The 7 Steps to a Worry-Free Retirement

A MUST READ FOR YOUNG AND ELDER RETIREES AND THE CHILDREN THAT LOVE THEM.

by **David L. Almond,** *CFP®, MSFS, MBA*

iUniverse, Inc.
New York Bloomington

The 7 Steps to a Worry-Free Retirement

A MUST READ FOR YOUNG AND ELDER RETIREES AND THE CHILDREN THAT LOVE THEM.

iUniverse books may be ordered through booksellers or by contacting:

iUniverse
1663 Liberty Drive
Bloomington, IN 47403
www.iuniverse.com
1-800-Authors (1-800-288-4677)

Because of the dynamic nature of the Internet, any Web addresses or links contained in this book may have changed since publication and may no longer be valid. The author is not engaged in rendering legal, tax, accounting, financial planning, investment, or similar professional services. Examples in this book are used for illustrative purposes only and do not represent recommendations or actual results. While legal, tax, accounting, financial planning, and investment issues covered in this book have been checked with sources believed to be reliable, some material may be affected by changes in the laws or in the interpretations of such laws since the manuscript for this book was completed. For that reason, the accuracy and completeness of such information and the opinions based thereon are not guaranteed. In addition, state or local tax laws or procedural rules may have a material impact on the general recommendations made by the author, and the strategies outlined in this book may not be suitable for every individual. The author encourages the reader to seek professional accounting, legal, tax, financial planning, and/or investment advice before implementing any of the strategies discussed in this book

ISBN: 978-0-595-52460-0 (pbk)
ISBN: 978-0-595-62512-3 (ebk)

iUniverse rev. date: 12/4/2008

Printed in the United States of America

What Others Are Saying About—The 7 Steps to a Worry-Free Retirement

"David Almond's experience and knowledge of the risks that retirees now face is unique. *The 7 Steps* is a great read for those who desire financial security in retirement."
—Ken Dychtwald, PhD, *author of The Power Years: A User's Guide to the Rest of Your Life*

"I have worked with Dave Almond for many years. His knowledge and professionalism in asset protection and planning for retirees is unsurpassed. For those that want to know how to protect themselves and their families from the *new retirement risk*, this book is a must read."
—Lisa N. Bertalan, *Estate Planning and Elder Law Attorney*

"David Almond cares about your financial security in retirement. If you want the advice of an experienced professional, this book is a gold mine!"
—Marilee Driscoll, *Author "The Complete Idiot's Guide to Long-term Care Planning," founder www.LTCmonth.com*

"For many years I have had the privilege of knowing Dave Almond both personally and professionally. I have referred many clients to Dave to assist them with their financial planning, particularly clients facing the enormous costs of long-term care. Dave's specialized knowledge in addressing the financial and personal challenges that face retirees and their families make him a valuable resource to my clients and my practice. Many of my clients have come to know Dave as a trusted advisor and friend, and hold him in high esteem. This book is an excellent resource for anyone who desires to understand the importance of financial planning for retirement."

— Phil Janney, *Estate Planning and Elder Law Attorney*

"Dave Almond's genuine caring and concern for retirees is reflected throughout this book in an easy to understand manner. This book is a MUST read for everyone who will retire someday, regardless of age. His honest approach to all facets of retirement options is refreshing."

—Bev Miller, CSA, CAS, *Benefits Division Manager; MainSource Insurance*

"Dave Almond's insight, applied in these uncertain times, will empower you to win in your golden years."

—J. Wesley Jackson, *President & Founder of Jackson Brokerage Corp.*

"An entertaining book on retirement planning that is easy to follow and written in an engrossing conversational style. I recommend it."

—Gordon K. Williamson, *Executive Director, Institute of Business & Finance*

" Wow! What a powerful How-To Guide…Dave Almond's book will benefit the new and seasoned advisor alike who share the desire to preserve our client's independence and dignity through the retirement years."

—Donald Garner, *Bank of Berne; Berne Financial Services*

"As a Long-Term Health Care professional, this is an excellent resource to read *prior* to moving to a retirement community. Navigating the Medicare, Medicaid and Managed Care systems is challenging and a wrong step can be costly. If you want to be in a position to make smart choices, this book is a "must read" for Boomers and their parents."

—Roberta Jacobsen, *President, Front Porch Communities and Services*

This book is dedicated to:

To my father Roy and my mother Zoe who loved, sacrificed for, and inspired me.

Also,

To the elders in our society who deserve our appreciation, honor, and respect. The younger generation will be blessed having sought their knowledge, wisdom, and experiences. "Gray hair is a crown of splendor; it is attained by a righteous life." -Proverbs 16:31

NINE THINGS THIS BOOK WILL HELP YOU ACHIEVE:

1. Protect your money against the cost of catastrophic illness with or without long-term care insurance.

2. Become an above average savvy investor.

3. Maintain your purchasing power for a long and uncertain retirement.

4. Create an income that you and/or your spouse cannot outlive.

5. Maintain your independence and dignity.

6. Stay in control of your financial future.

7. Keep from disinheriting yourself or your spouse.

8. Keep your money out of the hands of predators.

9. Achieve a worry-free retirement.

"Destiny is not a matter of chance it is a matter of choice."
-William Jennings Bryan

"My people are destroyed for a lack of knowledge."
-Hosea 4; 6

Contents

Acknowledgements

Profiting from their advice and inspired by their encouragement, I would like to thank the following people: My wife Pam for her loving support, counsel, and many contributions; Wes Jackson for his support, friendship, and encouragement; As a trailblazer on wealth transfer, John Becker for his counsel on the subject; Phil Janney and Lisa Bertalan for their contributions to my knowledge in this field and their helpful critique of this book; Marilee Driscoll for her direction and expertise; my daughter Linsy Almond for her positive attitude and many contributions; my niece Juliana Haley for her help and support. I would also like to give a special thanks to the following people for their contributions to my growth in helping retirees: Jean Gratteri, Daisy Doran, Gerry Heller, LaVerne Danko, Alice Brown, and Maxine Bischoff. To all of you I am very grateful.

Introduction

G o to any library, look on Amazon, or search on the web and you will find a myriad of books written on the subject of personal finance. So then why would I put my valuable time, resources, and energy into writing another book or for that matter think another financial book is even needed? And more important, why should you spend your valuable time to read it? Forty four years ago Bob Dylan wrote the song *These Times They Are A Changing.* As it pertains to our financial well being, Mr. Dylan's 1964 song rings true today. When it comes to change there is good news and bad news. *The good news is we will probably live longer than at any other time in history—the bad news is we have a greater chance of becoming financially destitute than at any other time in history.*

The National Bureau of Economic Research tells us that for millions of retirees, true financial security in retirement will prove an elusive goal. Dr. Ken Dychtwald , viewed as the leading authority on aging in America, states in his book *Age Power* that large numbers of elder boomers could wind up impoverished, and that we are woefully unprepared for what is about to occur as our population ages. If that isn't concerning enough, 54% of retirees surveyed had never thought about how many years they will spend in retirement and many are finding out that meeting the financial demands of living longer is proving to be more complicated than they envisioned. Moreover, a study conducted by Fidelity Investments tells us that 78% of those in retirement do not have a financial plan.

It used to be that a person would expect a relatively short life expectancy after retirement. Now many of us can plan on one third of our lives spent in retirement. Today retirees face a tremendous amount of financial uncertainty. The shift has changed from dying too soon to living too long—or what many experts define as a new financial problem: "longevity risk." The new challenge facing retirees today and tomorrow is how to provide income security for a long and uncertain retirement. To know if one will have enough money to last a lifetime is more important now than ever before.

Whereas retirees in the past could look to pensions to help provide for them through their golden years, corporations have increasingly removed much of the gold by making traditional defined pension plans almost extinct. Employers have exchanged them for plans that put the burden on the backs of the employee to save for their own future with plans like the ever popular 401(k) or 403(b), otherwise called defined contribution plans. If we are to depend on defined contribution plans to help us through a longer retirement period *than at any other time in history*, we must make smart investment choices. So how have we done over the last 19 years? From January of 1984 through December of 2002, the average investor received a return that did not even keep up with 3.14% annualized inflation. While the stock market as measured by the S&P 500 returned 12.22%, the average investor earned only 2.57%.

So why do some investors do better than others? Is it because they order the best newsletters? No! They have the best Stockbroker? Nonsense! The vast majority do better because they follow the principles identified in this book. We need to know the principles that successful investors use because one thing is for sure—the average investor is not prepared for the challenge ahead. Knowing how to invest is more critical than ever. Studies make it clear--if we want to be in control of our financial destiny, we have to become more savvy investors.

History sparkles with amusing examples of investment folly. The problem is instead of learning from them, we tend to repeat them, crippling our results, which in turn causes many of us to play it too safe. Playing it safe won't work! Because previous retirees did not spend as many years in retirement as we will, the traditional "safe" investment approach that we could get away with in the past, if used today, may in fact put current retirees and those retiring in the future at greater risk of running out of money.

As we look at making our money last, not only do we have to be savvy investors, but we must also be smart when it comes to generating income from our asset base (savings and investments), also called distribution planning. If we are to be equally savvy distribution planners, we must understand how to generate income that will last our lifetime. With a media that is focused more on how to accumulate money, distribution planning although equally important, gets little if any attention. Picking the hot stock or having the inside track on when to buy and when to sell is much more interesting to talk about at cocktail parties then how to produce income for a long and uncertain retirement. Although boring to some, I predict that in the near future, more emphasis will be placed on distribution planning because of necessity. But we can't wait for the media; we need answers *now* if we are to be successful.

While investing and distribution planning plays a critical role in the risk associated with living longer, if we are to achieve peace of mind in retirement, we can't ignore the #1 threat to our financial security and that is long-term care. Living longer brings with it financial landmines that can rob us of our financial dignity and independence, and long-term care is perhaps the greatest landmine. According to the American Health Care Association, "Failure to prepare for the cost of long-term care is the primary cause of impoverishment among the elderly." More than 50 percent of people age 65 and older will need long-term care before they pass away. Sadly, only 18 months after entering a nursing home, many residents are broke. This does not have to be! By knowing how to protect our assets from catastrophic illness, this statistic can and will change.

Another threat to our financial well being is the longer we live and the older we get, the odds are that we will be targeted by financial predators. Although noble when used for the benefits of those in need and for the care of our loved ones—*money*—when secured at any cost, can bring out the worst in some. In my humble opinion there is no greater "worst" then predators preying on our seniors. The Federal Trade Commission states that over 80 percent of telemarketing fraud victims are 65 or older. Nationally, from 2000 to 2001, reported incidents of identity theft involving victims over the age of 60 shot up by 218 percent in a single year! We must arm ourselves with information on how to fight this ongoing problem. Con criminals can erode our financial security leaving us dependent on family and/or the government.

Last but not least, finances have become more complicated. People often tell me, it used to be that in the past finances weren't so challenging and that dealing with money issues used to be easier and a lot less stressful. I agree and because of these complexities more retirees are seeking the advice of financial specialists. Unfortunately, some researchers tell us that many financial planners are not equipped to address and integrate the risks associated with longevity into their practices. Longevity risk brings with it the need for more specialized knowledge. Understandably, many financial advisors feel they serve the public better by staying with their core competencies such as investment management. While some planners have extended their practices to include distribution planning, most have chosen to stay away from integrating other important risks to living longer such as long-term care planning.

The approach to long-term care planning encompasses much more than just long-term care insurance and therefore is highly specialized. In my search for a planning tool that incorporated all of the risks associated with living longer, I could not find any that met my standards with the vast majority excluding long-term care planning altogether. You would think that every financial plan would take into account the #1 risk to financial security in retirement, but the fact is they don't. Out of necessity, I created my own planning analysis that incorporates all of the pieces to the longevity puzzle. Without addressing all of the risks that retirees are facing, we are left with only a flawed sense of security. Therefore, if retirees feel the need to get professional help, who they choose as their financial advisor (planner), can mean the difference of living a fulfilling and happy retirement or a dismal existence.

I have spent the last 22 years consulting with banks, giving public seminars, training other financial advisors, and serving my client's on the subjects contained in this book. As I have traveled around the country, I have met with hundreds of people about their money worries and concerns ranging from corporate executives to loving spouses whose husband or wife is in a long-term care facility. As I have shared principles in *The 7 steps* with those currently retired and those who are soon to be, I am moved by the responses that I have received. On several occasions I have been told their homes are much happier since planning their retirement years using the principles in this book. It is very satisfying to hear from people that have gone from worrying about their financial future to a greater level of peace in their lives. It means so much to me when clients say that I have helped them, or that I have made a positive difference. I also hear from those I have helped that they can sleep better and they are not fearful of their financial future.

I am honored that people in need of financial direction and clarity have put their trust in me. I am also honored by other professionals, be it an attorney, Certified Public Accountant (CPA) or other financial advisor, who refers their valued clients to me. Being selected as their advisor of choice to help them is something that I do not take lightly. Helping gives my life purpose and makes me feel important, but my journey did not start by jumping in and helping others. I, like other people I know, seem to have a common bond and that is we want to feel we have some control over our financial future. I started feeling this way many years ago. Sitting in my office at the restaurant that I owned frustrated with my newest tax bill, it dawned on me how little I knew about taxes, investing, insurance, and financial planning in general. That realization sent me on a mission to study and learn. (My wife calls me the consummate student. She often asks me, "Honey, when do you think that you will finally arrive?" My response is, "probably never because learning is enjoyable and helps me help others.")

I read a multitude of books, took college classes, immersed myself in home study courses, and eventually took and passed the required tests to secure my stockbroker and insurance license. I applied what I learned as a financial planner with American Express. My continued thirst for knowledge lead me to the College of Financial Planning where after years of study I became a Certified Financial Planner in 1989. I left American Express in 1989 with the desire to be independent.

The 7 Steps was not written from mere theory or guesswork, but from years of experience and real life cases. In this book you will meet people that probably share some of your concerns, fears, and goals. Like people in *The 7 Steps*, the subject matter is very close to me. My father suffered from Alzheimer's disease and passed away a few years ago. I know how it feels to experience the heartbreak of a disabled family member and the financial chaos it can bring. I have worked with many families over the years that have gone through and are going through the same thing. I have a compassion for families that are going through difficult times. It is hard enough to have a loved one in a long-term care facility or lose someone close to us without the added stress of worrying about running out of money. And even if we haven't lost a loved one or if a family member doesn't need care, from my experience when it comes to money, we still tend to worry about the future. Will we have enough…and what if this…and what if that?

I wrote *The 7 Steps* with the sole purpose of empowering retirees, and the families of those who love them, to live just that…a worry-free retirement no matter the circumstances. Although longevity risk brings with it new challenges, I believe that the keys to overcome these new challenges are contained in this book. In order to guard yourself against the new retirement risk you will need to know and put into action the information presented in each chapter. Here is a brief summary of what you can expect to learn:

In *Chapter 1* I will show you how to become an above average investor and what you need to know to stave off longevity risk.

Chapter 2 will teach you about the only investment option that can accomplish all of the following:

1. Protect your money from catastrophic illness.
2. Make the government your partner in accumulation and distribution, and:
3. Provide you with a pension that you and your spouse cannot outlive

In *Chapter 3* you will learn how simple it is to build worry-free income using the principles in Chapters 1 and 2.

Chapter 4 will tell you what few people know about how to protect yourself and aging parents from the #1 risk to your financial security and it will inspire you to help others.

Chapter 5 will give you tools to help protect yourself and your family from becoming the victim of financial perpetrators.

Chapter 6 will tell you what you need to know if you decide not to go it alone and opt to hire a financial advisor.

Chapter 7 will help you navigate the current retirement waters.

If we are to meet the new retirement challenge—living our years in comfort and not becoming dependent on loved ones and/ or the government—we need the keys that will unlock the answers to longevity risk. *The 7 Steps* will give you the answers that you need to stop worrying and start enjoying your retirement years. From my research, it is the only book that takes a *holistic approach* to the risks associated with living longer and gives easy to follow steps to defeat those risks. Even if you are not retired but have retired parents, your family will appreciate you for stepping up and learning the information contained in this book so you can help them with confidence and conviction. It is my prayer that this book gives you peace of mind. Also, that it empowers you to take control and stay in control of your financial future. I am confident that it will, which makes it worth the time and effort to bring it to you. May God bless you.

Chapter 1

Investing to Help Make Your Money Last a Lifetime

The First Step to a Worry-Free Retirement

"Those who do not remember the past are condemned to repeat it."
Santayana

C urrent studies show that investment practices of the past may not be adequate to meet the new retirement challenge. A traditional conservative portfolio that was sufficient for previous retirees—if used today—may put current retirees, and those retiring in the future, at risk of running out of money. If we knew with certainty how long we will live, it would be fairly easy to invest our savings to meet the needs of our remaining years on this earth. But since we don't know how long we will live, understanding how to invest our hard earned money for a long and uncertain period of time becomes a critical issue. Research has left little doubt, that living longer necessitates the need to become an informed investor if we are to control our financial destiny.

Although past investment results are no guarantee of future performance, the markets have provided observers a measure of predictability. We only have the past to look at when making decisions for the present as well as the future. Educating ourselves about how asset classes have preformed over time, will help us make smart investment choices.

Besides being a smart investor and understanding investment history, if we desire financial security, we must stay in control of our behavior. The wrong behavior can have a major affect on our investment success. We may not even know if we are acting rationally or irrationally when it comes to investing. Fear of loss, especially in retirement when

> *But since we don't know how long we will live, understanding how to invest our hard earned money for a long and uncertain period of time becomes a critical issue.*

it is difficult, if not impossible, to regain money lost from bad investment decisions, is an emotion that I have seen over and over again in my 22 years of helping people. Fear is often the driving force behind acting irrationally. If you are one that is held back by fear, you can take refuge in the fact that the information in this chapter will help give you the tools to defeat your fear. If you are to move from fear that may be holding you back, to conquest, you will need to have an understanding of the following keys to successful investing as we move into a new time in history. We must know:

1. The importance of maintaining purchasing power and how to accomplish it.
2. How to put together an asset allocation model based on need, risk tolerance, and time horizon.
3. Investor behavior and how to guard ourselves from the wrong actions.

MAINTAINING PURCHASING **POWER**

Now at age 54, I can remember when 25 cents would buy a bunch of candy. (When I was little, I actually would dream about candy falling from the sky. I'm glad I grew out of that.) In 6th grade I begged my parents to buy me the coolest tennis shoes (we always called them tennis shoes…never sneakers). The coolest tennis shoes at that time were Converse. Because my parents loved me and they were intent on peace and quiet in the house, they gave in and bought me a pair, which cost $10. Unfortunately, the day of cool tennis shoes for $10 is long gone.

As inflation has always been a part of our lives, due to living longer, inflation is a greater threat to our financial health now more than at any other time in history. If inflation were to average 4% per year, it would reduce the purchasing power of a $100,000 annual income to less than $68,000 in just 10 years. That equates to about 1/3 reduction in purchasing power every 10 years. With a 25 year increase in life expectancy, you get the picture. Therefore, *if our investment portfolio does not take inflation into account, we may put ourselves at greater risk of reducing our standard of living and possibly depleting our assets thus becoming financially dependent on family, government or both.*

Wharton finance professor <u>Richard Marston</u>, who directs a program on <u>private wealth management</u> at Wharton, notes two fundamental issues investors must address. These issues are living longer, and how much one expects to spend every year in retirement. Professor Marston makes the important point that we must balance our

> *As inflation has always been a part of our lives, due to living longer, inflation is a greater threat to our financial health now more than at any other time in history.*

spending needs with the probable returns on our portfolio. If out of balance, we are at risk of running out of money before running out of life.

An economist for AARP, Clare Hushbeck states "Inflation can really kill an income stream after 20 years. It can represent a definite threat to individuals in retirement". Joining the chorus, Money magazine published an article in 1993 that identified inflation as one of five distinct threats to a successful retirement. The article went on to say, retirees may find it necessary to take on more risk in their investment portfolios if they desire to maintain their standard of living. A distinct relationship exists between purchasing power and inflation that cannot be ignored especially when faced with longer life expectancies.

In order to help eliminate the effects of inflation, stock ownership will play a more important role for future retirees then those that retired in the past. I am not talking about purchasing individual stocks necessarily, but rather understanding the need to have some equity ownership in our portfolio. If you are asking, "How much equity ownership are you talking about?" I wish I could answer that to give you some peace of mind but I cannot. Everyone is unique and we all have our own financial fingerprint.

I know from experience that many retirees do not like the thought of owning stocks. Haunting many is the fact that most cannot afford a financial setback. The fear of investing in stocks and the possibility of losing money is crippling to some. Studies support the fact that investors are less willing to take financial risk as they age and the result is less stock holdings. First of all, we have to come to grips with the fact that owning an inflation hedge, such as stocks, doesn't increase our risk—as it pertains to living longer—it actually decreases it. The fact is, adding some stocks to an all bond portfolio (which most believe is less risky than owning any stocks), in reality reduces risk. The good news is, as we better understand how stock ownership can help us, and how to invest our money wisely, our fears can be replaced with confidence.

Life teaches us that risk is part of living and investing is no different. We can never completely eliminate risk in life or when investing. Once we better understand that we always face risk in one form or the other, we are in a position to better control it, instead of it controlling us. *As it relates to inflation, burying our money in the back yard, putting it under our mattress, or putting everything in "accounts that are guaranteed" to help avoid the risk of losing it, may possibly be the worst thing we can do.* We might still be able to go to our back yard and dig up our money, but like

> *Life teaches us that risk is part of living and investing is no different. We can never completely eliminate risk in life nor when investing.*

anything buried, it starts to lose its luster both in looks and what kind of lifestyle it can provide. We have in fact traded the risk of losing a tangible piece of paper for the possibility of a less comfortable lifestyle. Therefore, be it either burying our money in the back yard or burying our heads in the sand, we cannot get away from risk altogether. There are several types of risks when it comes to our money, but as we live longer, retirees will have to come to grips with the tradeoff between two forms of risk which are:

- Purchasing power risk, which comes from putting all our money in what we believe are "risk free" investments such as certificate of deposits, certain bonds, burying our money in the back yard or putting it under our pillow.
- Market risk, which is defined by a key risk we expose ourselves to when we buy stocks.

The new retirement challenge of living longer puts us in a position of deciding between maintaining a specified standard of living and how much risk we need to take in order to achieve it. *The secret is, knowing how to take as little risk as possible in order to achieve the investment return on our money that we need to support our lifestyle.* You are probably asking (I know I would), how do I determine how much return I need in order to find out how much risk I have to take? Good question. Here is the answer; you or your advisor will need to:

1.   Figure your expenses inflated over your life expectancy (include irregular expenses such as buying a new car, furniture, future events, etc.)

2. Gather all sources of income with cost of living increases if they have any; determine when and if any income sources will end and if so, when.

3. Take inventory of your investment assets and any other assets that currently do not generate income that you may convert to income producing assets in the future.

4. Figure the most efficient way to take income which should focus on the net, not the gross. *It is not what you make but what you keep that matters.* From there, figure your after tax return on all income.

5. Take into account how you will pay for long-term care if one or both of you need it in the future.

6. Determine your investment mix which will show you the risk that you may need to take to meet your income needs.

Once you determine the return that you need—and if you want to reduce your financial risk—here are nine things you can do to help drive down risk. They are:

1. Lower your income needs.

2. Work part time for additional income.

3. Delay retirement (unless you are already retired).

4. Tap the equity in your home through the use of a reverse mortgage (there are qualifications for this strategy which I cover in Chapter 4).

5. Insure against the number one threat to financial security in retirement which is long-term care.

6. Create your own income pension by using a life income annuity that you cannot outlive (I cover this in more detail in Chapters 2 & 3).

7. Create more tax efficient income.

8. Separate your money into buckets based on time frame…short term buckets with no market risk moving to long-term buckets with some market risks…the long-term buckets being the inflation hedge buckets.

9. Use an efficient frontier allocation model for your long-term equity buckets which I will share with you next.

Now we know we must protect our money from the ravages of inflation as well as market risk. The next step is to educate ourselves on the smart way to investment in order to help accomplish these two objectives. Asset allocation is a tried and proven investment system that can help us realize our goal.

ASSET ALLOCATION

Time to test your investment savvy; how would you answer this question? Which of the following is/are the greatest contributor(s) to ones' success as an investor?

a. Knowing how to time the market.

b. Asset allocation

c. The stocks and bonds that you select for your portfolio.

> *Asset allocation accounts for over 93.6 percent of the return variability among the funds, with a less-than-7 percent contribution from market timing and actual stock and bond selection.*

Okay, that was pretty easy! You probably knew from the heading of this chapter that the answer is b. Asset allocation is more important to your investment success then stock picking or timing the market! Two sophisticated statistical studies of 82 large pension funds concluded that asset allocation accounted for over 93.6 percent of the return variability among the funds, with a less-than-7 percent contribution from market timing and actual stock and bond selection.[10] A study conducted by Lummer and Riepe in 1994 concluded that "Asset allocation is therefore the most fundamental of investment decisions."

In the not very distant past, asset allocation was not available to the average investor. It belonged to the closed club of Wall Street big wigs. (The older I get and the more hair that I lose, the more I dislike the term "big wigs.") Once asset allocation made it to Main Street, the models only addressed basic functions of dividing money between assets based on factors such as age, income, dependents, and the like. Today, asset allocation is a far more rigorous enterprise involving the use of sophisticated tools that have transformed the process. Asset allocation models have grown leaps and bounds in their ability to help the average investor. Through the use of asset allocation, we stack the deck in our favor in our quest to become smart investors. We now have at our disposal the tools that have made the greatest contribution to the success of big pension plans and investment gurus.

WHAT IS ASSET ALLOCATION?

Let's say you owned stock in Sears and you wanted to diversify to guard against having all of your eggs in one basket. You decide to spread your risk by purchasing stock in Dell and Microsoft. The theory goes that if Sears fell on bad times, hopefully Dell and Microsoft would perform well and help guard against a loss in your overall portfolio. The problem is that if the stock market dropped, more than likely all of the stocks that you owned would probably also drop. As the saying goes, "all boats rise with the tide" and in the case of stocks, they usually fall with the tide. Therefore, if your investments only consisted of Dell, Microsoft, and Sears, your portfolio would be void of any investments that would help counterbalance the drop in the market. In other words, you may have diversified a little by owning more than one stock, but you haven't helped protect your investments from going south when the market does.

So what do we do to help protect our self from such a fate? Enter—*asset allocation*. Asset allocation is a means of diversifying one's investment dollars among various asset classes in such a way as to minimize overall risk and enhance overall return. Asset allocation involves diversifying investments among all or some of the primary asset categories as shown below:

➤ Cash & Cash Equivalents
➤ Domestic Stocks
  o Large Cap Market
  o Large Cap Value
  o Mid Cap Market
  o Mid Cap Value
  o Small Cap Market
  o Small Cap Value
➤ International Stocks
  o Large Cap Market
  o Large Cap Value
  o Mid Cap Market
  o Mid Cap Value
  o Small Cap Market
  o Small Cap Value

- o Emerging Market-Market
- o Emerging Market Value
- o Emerging Market Small Cap
- ➤ Fixed Income: Domestic and International
- o Short Term Bonds
- o Intermediate Term Bonds
- o (I am purposely leaving out long-term bonds— the risk to return has been historically too high)
- ➤ Real Estate
- ➤ Precious Metals such as Gold and Silver

In the 1950s, Harry Markowitz developed the basic underpinnings of asset allocation theories commonly accepted today. Mr. Markowitz theory awarded him a share of the 1990 Nobel Prize in Economics. His findings helped the investment community understand to a greater degree the relationship between risk and return. Any portfolio can be plotted on a graph. Graph 1 shows "return" moving up and down, while "risk" moves left to right.

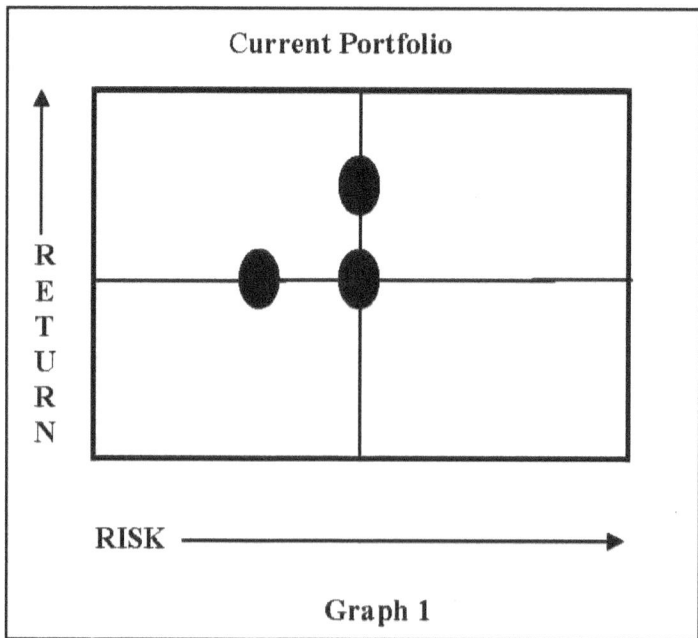

The circle in the center at the intersection of the two lines represents a portfolio and how it fares in relation to risk and return. The objective is to accomplish one of two things: 1) achieving a higher return (as shown by the top circle) at the same risk currently taken; or 2) moving to the left on the risk line (the circle to the left) to achieve the same return while reducing risk. A combination of any of the two improves the risk and reward relationship. How is this accomplished? Graph 2 represents time and return.

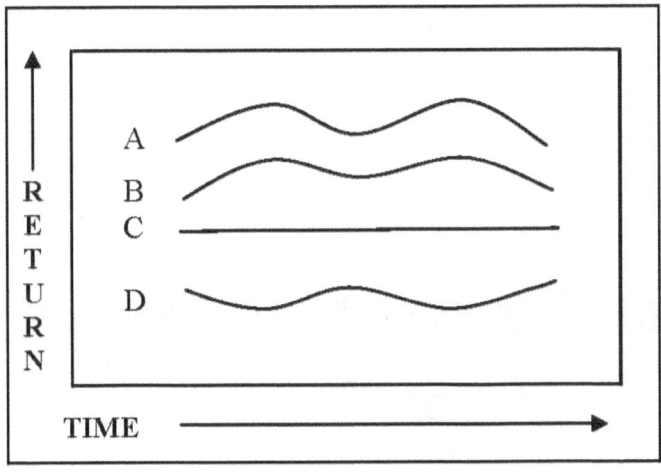

Graph 2

We can examine how assets have acted historically. If assets move in tandem (assets A & B), then we don't have the correct relationship between risk and return. By strategically adding assets that move counter to each other (assets B & D) to the portfolio, then we are able to smooth out volatility (shown by line C), squeezing out the risk while working to accomplish the return needed for financial independence. Designing a portfolio using this strategy will help achieve a higher return without taking on more risk or lowering the risk while achieving the same return that we were getting from the previous portfolio.

> *By strategically adding assets that move counter to each other to the portfolio, then we are able to smooth out volatility, squeezing out the risk while working to accomplish the return needed for financial independence.*

WHY NOT JUST PICK A GOOD MUTUAL FUND

You may be asking yourself, "Why do I need asset allocation? Why not just pick a good mutual fund?" While that may be better than doing nothing, it does little to help us accomplish our goal of either lowering risk while achieving the same return, or keeping the same level of risk while increasing our return. If we take a look at Graph 3, we will notice that a hot asset class one year is not necessarily at the top of the heap the following year—and certainly not on top all of the time. Take International stocks for example; you can see that from 1986 through 1988, they were the top performing stocks. Then look at where they placed from 1990 through 1995. Be it a stock, mutual fund, or asset class, investing in what was hot yesterday or today fuels the fires of buying high and selling low. Why?—because what is on top today will spend time on the bottom tomorrow, and once it starts sliding downward it becomes easy to panic and sell. Second, owning a single mutual fund does not accomplish our goal of owning assets that move counter to each other helping us smooth out volatility.

Asset Class Winners and Losers

	1986	1987	1988	1989	1990	1991	1992	1993	1994	1995	1996	1997	1998	1999	2000
HIGHEST RETURN	Internat'l Stocks			Large Stocks	30 Day T-Bills		Small Stocks	Internat'l Stocks			Large Stocks			Small Stocks	LT Gov't Bonds
	LT Gov't Bonds	30 Day T-Bills	Small Stocks		LT Gov't Bonds	Large Stocks	LT Gov't Bonds	Small Stocks	30 Day T-Bills		Small Stocks		Internat'l Stocks	30 Day T-Bills
		Large Stocks		Internat'l Stocks	Large Stocks	LT Gov't Bonds	Large Stocks	LT Gov't Bonds	Small Stocks	LT Gov't Bonds	Internat'l Stocks	LT Gov't Bonds		Large Stocks	Small Stocks
	Small Stocks	LT Gov't Bonds		Small Stocks		Internat'l Stocks	30 Day T-Bills	Large Stocks	Internat'l Stocks		30 Day T-Bills			Large Stocks
LOWEST RETURN	30 Day T-Bills	Small Stocks	30 Day T-Bills	Internat'l Stocks	30 Day T-Bills	Internat'l Stocks	30 Day T-Bills	LT Gov't Bonds	30 Day T-Bills	LT Gov't Bonds	Internat'l Stocks	Small Stocks	LT Gov't Bonds	Internat'l Stocks

Graph 3

Another reasonable question would be, "Can't I just pick a seasoned mutual fund manager who can solve the problem of being on top one year and being on bottom in following years?" That doesn't work either! In 1968, Michael Jensen published a paper in the Journal of Finance, and his findings were that in a 20 year period from 1945 to 1964, he could find no evidence of persistent performance by mutual fund managers. Last year's top managers didn't stay there long and ultimately their performance showed mediocre results. Recent studies that have followed support Mr. Jensen's findings.

Not only is it difficult, if not impossible, for a mutual fund manager to outperform his or her peers, but as it relates to staying on top, they also have another problem—which is, in most cases, the fund objective limits how they can invest. What do I mean by "limits how they can invest?" Take for instance a mutual fund that invests in "large stocks." If the primary fund objective is to

> *A hot asset class one year is not necessarily at the top of the heap the following year—and certainly not on top all of the time.*

invest in large stocks, then the manager is restricted and can only invest in what is allowed and in this case—it is large stocks. Once again looking at Graph 3, we can see that, no matter how good the fund manager, when large stocks are out of favor, that fund's return is going to suffer. The message is clear—we cannot just pick a hot mutual fund expecting it to save the day. If you do so you will be under-water much of the time, trying to swim upstream against the financial currents.

There is also another problem with this approach to investing. Studies show that those that buy the "hot funds" usually do so because they are chasing performance. When one chases performance, it is because the fund has done well and it is either on the climb or it has already peaked, and you guessed it—it is on its way down. The ride down is the ride that most investors take. The following statement cannot be said enough, and that is—*if we are to be an above average investor, we cannot fall in the trap of buying high and selling low*—and picking a hot fund increases the chance of buying at the wrong time. Fortunately, a properly designed asset allocation model, if we stick with it, helps us avoid this trap.

Although it is not smart to simply pick a hot fund or manager, we will nevertheless need to select specific mutual fund type investments that represent asset classes needed to build our asset allocation model(s). As we do so, one is well served to guard against falling prey to "style drift" and "overlap." Either can derail your asset allocation model. Let's first look at style drift: Style drift is a problem when a money manager who's supposed to be investing only in a certain asset type, such as blue-chip stocks, puts some of the fund's money into another asset type, such as small-company stocks. As such, your asset allocation percentages can be askew possibly adding unwanted risk to your portfolio.

Next, let's look at overlap. Overlap exists when the same stock is owned by some or all of the mutual funds in your portfolio. Let's say that you have two balanced funds, two large cap technology funds, one large cap growth fund, and one large cap value fund that are managed by different mutual fund companies. You purchased these different funds because you want to be diversified. You find out from checking the semiannual or annual reports that they all have IBM, Microsoft, and Dell as major holdings. Many of the most popular equity mutual funds own the same companies. Therefore, even though you have invested in various mutual funds, you may not be as diversified as you thought due to the fact that those funds have a concentrated amount of their money invested in the same companies, thus creating overlap. An effective way to guard against "style drift and overlap" is to use index funds. Index funds are not actively managed which eliminates the problem of "style drift and overlap".

PROPER ASSET ALLOCATION BASED ON NEED, RISK TOLERANCE, AND TIME HORIZON

"In tennis as well as investing, success is less a matter of winning than avoiding losing. The ultimate loss-avoidance strategy, then, is to simply buy and hold." Charles Ellis, 1972 Journal of Finance

As I have talked about in this chapter, the objective should be to achieve our desired investment return while taking as little risk as possible. Another way we can go about reducing risk

The objective should be to achieve our desired investment return while taking as little risk as possible. History has shown, the longer an investor has to reach his or her goal, the less risky any given course of action is.

is by putting time on our side. History has shown, the longer an investor has to reach his or her goal, the less risky any given course of action is. Stated another way, the longer an investor's time horizon, the more aggressive he or she can be. This is because, the longer the horizon, the more time the investor has to make up for losses, and/or to compound gains. Let's look at some historical facts that give us some predictability when it comes to investing in asset classes. Keep in mind that past performance does not guarantee future performance. If future performance could be guaranteed by past performance, we wouldn't need an asset allocation model; we would simply put all of our money in the asset class that has provided the best historical results.

Graph 4 shows that over the long-term stocks have been the best place to put our money. In real-dollar terms (adjusted for inflation), large U.S. stocks have outperformed bonds and cash investments in terms of total return. A $1.00 investment, 81 years ago, in the stock market measured by the S&P 500, would have grown to $271.72 by the end of 2005. The same $1.00 invested in long U.S. government treasury bonds for those 81 years would be worth $5.77. $1.00 invested in U.S. long-term corporate bonds for the same time period did slightly better than treasury bonds and would be worth about $8.89, while T-Bills would have returned $1.72. The returns above are adjusted for inflation so these are real returns. They also assume tax-free investments (with taxes the growth would be less dramatic but would be even more in favor of stocks given the lower tax rates on capital gains and dividends).

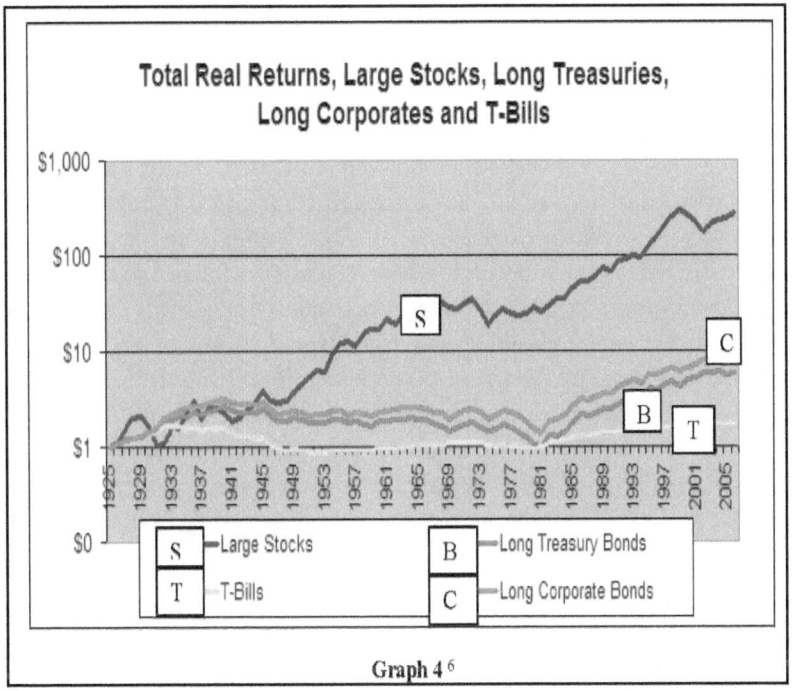

Graph 4 [6]

Historically, investing over longer periods of time has actually reduced the risk of loss. *In fact, while the market has suffered 23 losing years since 1926, there has never been a 15-year period when the stock market lost value.*[6] The record illustrates the importance of maintaining a long-term perspective, rather than panicking and then selling an investment during market downturns. Studies show that if we can buy and hold, we can ride out the stock market volatility, helping us maintain our purchasing power. So what is the answer to designing a portfolio to guard against longevity risk? The answer is to design separate portfolios based on income needs and time horizons—putting money into buckets per say. Each bucket is given a period to grow and then to distribute income. The short-term buckets are conservative and therefore use conservative investments with no or low volatility. The longer term buckets are less conservative and therefore contain an asset allocation model designed to help guard against a decline in purchasing power. While the short-term buckets may include little to no stocks, the longer term buckets would have an increased amount of stocks based on how many years until that bucket is needed to produce income.

The bucket approach helps us take advantage of the buy and hold strategy and also helps protect us against irrational behavior. I will give you an example from a client who is a young retiree I will call

The answer is, to design separate portfolios based on income needs and time horizons—-putting money into buckets per say

Sally. Sally is healthy and should have many years to enjoy her grandchildren and active lifestyle. Sally called me one day and said "David, I heard on the news that the outlook for the stock market is not good. I spoke with a few friends and they confirmed that now is a good time to sell and get out." I responded, "Sally, remember that when we did your plan, the only buckets that have any stocks in them will not be needed to provide income for at least 15 years. Don't worry about short-term ups and downs of the market; we know that if you are to meet your income and lifestyle needs, it is important that your stocks are left for the long-term to help offset inflation. I don't want you to miss the returns that the market has historically produced. One way to miss the return is to sell low, when stocks are down, and buy them back when they are up. That is exactly the opposite of what a savvy investor does. We need to stay the course." Sally needed for me to reassure her so she wouldn't worry.

Following the advice of the media and friends, contributes to the fact that so many people become average or below average investors and do not achieve the returns that they would if they stayed on track. Sometimes, your financial advisor's job is to help you chart the course and stay with the ship when the waters get rough. The worst thing we can do is get off course.

We have learned that we need to "inflation proof" our investment portfolio and that asset allocation is important if we are to lower risk while achieving the desired return. What else can keep us from achieving success? It is called *investor behavior*. Investor behavior is a key reason why most people achieve average or below average results. While some of the negative behaviors are influenced by our emotions, some are knowledge based, meaning we simply don't know what we don't know. If we are to become above average investors, we must be aware of these behaviors and we also must be in control of our emotions. Regarding our emotions, I am not picking on any of us, the Lord knows that our emotions can get the best of us at times, but knowing these behaviors and how to guard against them can give us confidence in times of doubt. Here is a look at some of the most common behaviors that can cause us problems.

If we are to become above average investors, we must be aware of these behaviors and we also must be in control of our emotions.

UNDERSTANDING BEHAVIORS THAT CAN GET IN THE WAY OF INVESTMENT SUCCESS

Russ and Joann were referred to me by a client. Like many couples, spouses do not always agree on how to invest their money. Often one spouse is more conservative than the other. This meeting was no different. Joann was disappointed because Russ was not willing to invest their money in anything that he felt had risk. Being their second marriage, each had different views on how to invest money. Russ wanted nothing to do with stocks and Joann disagreed. She was convinced that stocks were necessary if they were going to live in the style that she had become accustomed. Joann had invested in stocks through her 401(k) and had done reasonably well while Russ's money was inherited from the recent passing of his mother. Russ remembered the stories his father told about losing money in the stock market. Russ got the message—if he had any sense he would stay away from such folly. While Joann knew that she could invest her money separate from Russ, she loved him and wanted them to agree on where and how they should invest. While Joann had some frustration, she was not judgmental of Russ and even understood his hesitation. Joann was hoping that I could waylay Russ's fears. Rational or irrational, fears are fears and they can be paralyzing for all of us.

I asked Russ if he could tell me more about his family's experiences investing in stocks. He spoke with intense passion, "Back in 1987 my father had just put several thousands of dollars in the stock market and on ... I believe it was called black Monday, he lost a lot of money. It was devastating to my family. My father was so confident that it was the right thing to do at the time because a friend of his had made some good money with a certain mutual fund. I can't recall the name of it but his friend was always talking about how much money he was making. There is no way that I can live through that again. I wish that I had Joann's confidence but I just don't."

I remember that day well. I was in my office and the national fallout was devastating. Many stockbrokers, financial planners, and investment advisors, would not answer their phones because of the panic. News of brokers being shot and investors committing suicide was heard around the country. On that Monday, October 19, 1987, the Dow Jones Industrial Average fell 508.32 and closed at a record-breaking low of 1,738.40 points. This date, now known to the world as Black Monday, is documented as the worst stock market crash in history. The 22.9% loss in 1987 almost doubles the percentage lost in the Crash of 1929, which was 12.82%. That experience would be hard for anyone to risk repeating. My heart went out to Russ.

The crash was blamed on portfolio insurance, program trading, and the fact that many investors moved their money to 30 year US bonds that were yielding 10%. Although the effects of the Crash of 1987 were not as devastating as expected, it nonetheless shook the confidence of investors. Like many market corrections, it actually became *a marvelous buying opportunity.* In the following decade, investors displayed a renewed trust in the market. The public returned to the market as it made a comeback and began to rise.

If we follow the stock market history, we see from experience that the market acted in 1987 like it always does. It is like a roller coaster, it goes up and down in varying degrees. If we don't understand this fact, we are likely to jump off at the worst time. History has given us some predictability. If we ride it out, and don't jump; the deck is stacked in our favor that we will come out ahead. To support my point, the S&P 500 from January 1984 through December of 2002, provided an average annual return of 12.22%. What does that tell us? Those that *did not* jump in 1987 and stayed the course fared much better than the average investor that only achieved a 2.57% return during the same time period.

If we look at historical market corrections, the market is doing what it always does. That is, when it is overpriced, it is only a matter of time until the price of stocks come back in line with reality. We as investors exacerbate the market swings by acting irrationally. What do I mean by acting irrationally? Take for example buying clothes or furniture; don't we usually look for sales before we buy them? Unless we need the money right now, wouldn't we hesitate from selling something if we can't sell it for what it is worth? Applying that same rational thinking to the stock market, we

> *We as investors exacerbate the market swings by acting irrationally.*

would do the opposite of what most investors do and that is we would buy when the market is dropping and sell when it is rising. Let me just say, acting rationally in a time of fear or panic is not easy. If we cut our self and the cut is not life threatening, but none the less scary, the worst thing we can do is panic because that makes our heart pump faster which in turn makes the problem worse. Investing is much the same, we stand a better chance of staying out of the financial ER if we do not panic, but instead behave rationally.

Irrational behavior may cause financial hemorrhaging. Rational behavior would be to buy when stocks are cheap and sell when they are expensive. Easier said than done and that is why investors have had the best results from the strategy of buying and holding for the long-term. While I am on the subject, if rational investing is your goal, you will want to screen the financial publications and programs that you read or watch. Some financial professionals, with the intent of selling magazines and/or air time, intentionally try to fuel the irrational fires. They do so by instructing people to try and time the market …when to get in and when to get out…also, by promoting investment products by pushing only the upside and not the downside. A word of caution: if a person who gives financial advice makes what they are selling sound too good to be true and only talks about the high returns (the upside), do yourself a favor and change the channel or change your advisor. You will thank me for it, and you will be in a better position to keep your hard earned money.

As we look at investor behavior, we can benefit by taking to heart the sound advice, "Those who do not remember the past are condemned to repeat it." With the stellar market performance of the 1990s, many of us forgot the lesson of 1987. Those of us who forgot were reminded in the year 2000. Irrational behavior is nothing new; it has been around since the fall of Adam and Eve. A book that I read years ago and highly recommend is titled *Extraordinary Popular Delusions and the Madness of Crowds* by Charles Mackay. First published in 1841, Mr. Mackay chronicles investor behavior dating back over the course of history.

Mr. Mackay's objective was to show how easily the masses have been led astray. If we would have taken Mr. Mackay's teachings to heart, many may have been saved from repeating the speculative bubbles of the past and possibly could have recognized that the bubble was once again alive and well prior to the year 2000. It is no wonder then that research shows proper investing is far more dependent on investor behavior than on investment performance. Here are some investor behaviors that we are well served to avoid.

> *It is no wonder then that research shows proper investing is far more dependent on investor behavior than on investment performance.*

Behavior #1…*Expecting High Returns with Low Risk*. Russ's father fell victim to this behavior. He had expected high returns because his friend had experienced them. What he didn't take into account was the risk that he exposed himself to. For that reason, Russ's father was more of a speculator then an investor. An investor is going to look at the risk/return relationship before diving head first into the deep end. Jumping in without taking into account financial and historical data falls in the speculative arena as opposed to the investment arena. An important note: anytime an advisor recommends a specific investment, ask them for the Standard Deviation of annual returns. If they cannot tell you, I would recommend that you look for another advisor. If Russ's father had an understanding of the risk/return relationship of his investment, he would have been in a better position to make an informed decision.

Behavior #2...*Following the Herd.* "Where all think alike, no one thinks very much."—Walter Lippman. Following the herd sounds demeaning to us as people, but as I pointed out, if we follow the historical patterns of behavior, many investors fall victim to what is called herding or also known as "social proof." In his book, *Influence... The Psychology of Persuasion,* Robert B. Cialdini, PH.D, provides us with an understanding of herding by using canned laughter as an example. Television executives, although knowing that most audiences find canned laughter stupid, phony, and obvious, use it anyway. The reason being that executives discovered we, as people, use herding or social proof to help take what we believe is the correct action. In other words, *if others think it is correct then it must be.*

Dr. Cialdini's research supports an investment behavior that has plagued us for centuries—we tend to see an action as appropriate if someone else is doing it. Familiarity with "herding", and how it affects our decisions will help us guard against taking someone else's word for our investment choices. We are then less likely to follow the crowd and get caught up in the bubble frenzy and make investment decisions that do not benefit us personally. Understanding the principles of herding should guard us from assuming that if someone else has put their money in a certain investment, they must have done their homework, and therefore we do not have to check it out for ourselves. History as a reminder tells us that poor investment decisions would be largely curtailed if investors didn't follow the crowd. Russ's father would have saved himself and his family a lot of grief, if he wouldn't have assumed that his friend had done his homework and he had done his own.

Behavior #3 ...*Overconfidence.* "No problem in judgment and decision making is more prevalent and more potentially catastrophic than overconfidence."—Plous (1993). Psychologists tell us that people tend to be overconfident. The more complex the task, the more overconfident we tend to be. We can become vulnerable by overestimating our knowledge, underestimating the risks, and tending to believe that we have more control over events than we actually do. Overconfidence when it comes to investing can be dangerous because investing can be a complex task. An example of overconfidence is one study polling a group of new business owners; showed that 81% of which thought that they had a good chance of succeeding, but in turn thought only 39% of their peers would succeed. How does overconfidence manifest itself in making investment decisions?

- We think that our returns will be higher than the facts support.

- Active trading thinking that we can beat the market—research supports that this type of behavior most often benefits the broker/advisor more than the client.

- Contributing to speculative bubbles as previously discussed.

What we don't know can hurt us. We can guard against overconfidence by becoming an informed investor which leads me to the next behavior.

Behavior #4...*Investing in things we don't understand.* Over the years I've met with clients who, as they're handing me a product statement from a company, say to me, "I have my money in a (certain product). Can you explain how it works?" Granted, people may forget what they've invested in, but many times they've purchased something because a friend owned it, or they simply trusted their agent or rep to decide for them. An investment should fit your needs. In order to determine that it does, you should have a working understanding of what it is and how it works. If your agent or rep uses financial jargon or cannot explain the recommendation in terms that you can understand, consider working with someone else who can communicate to your satisfaction.

If you have a hard time understanding financial issues, consider asking a family member or a trusted friend to sit in on the meetings to assist you. Another person who understands your communication style might enable you to make more informed decisions. You shouldn't have to know everything about a specific investment, but you should have enough information to make an informed decision.

Behavior #5...*Recency.* Recency helps explain investor results. Our expectations are based on what stocks have done in recent times and we forget about long-term performance. We tend to think that if the market provided a return of 20% over the last five years, we should expect the same return over the next five years. Recency sets us up for failure. We can become disillusioned when the results are not what we expected, motivating us to change course. Some might say this is because of the need for immediate gratification or that we are impatient. Either way, we need to embrace the fact that successful investors take a long-term approach. Knowing how recency can affect our overall results will help us guard against focusing on the short-term as opposed to what we should do which is take a long-term view.

Behavior #6...*Trying to Time the Stock Market.* There is a difference between investing in stocks and trying to time the market. The former is equity ownership in a company. The latter is trying to make money based on the movement of the market. Many publications and news programs talk about when to get in and out. Don't be fooled—even the pros can't time the market successfully. Researchers John Graham and Campbell Harvy conducted a study and found that 237 newsletter guru's telling investors when to put their money in the market and when to take it out, were right less than 25% of the time. Even worse, not one advisor out of all 237 was consistently correct and many were wrong on a regular basis. Most experts agree, if you want

> *Historically, investors have fared better when they have invested for the long-term. "Mutual Fund investors who hold their investments are more successful than those that time the market."*

to underperform the market 7 out of 10 times, *try to time it.* So next time you hear someone on the news, or in your circle of friends and/or family tell you that it may be time to get out of stocks because of the market outlook… think again. Historically, investors have fared better when they have invested for the long-term. "Mutual Fund investors who hold their investments are more successful than those that time the market."[5]

Behavior #7…*Making Decisions Without Considering All Implications.* My experience and education confirms to me that no matter how smart or how long your financial advisor has been in the business, he cannot with relative confidence, recommend an investment portfolio without knowing several factors such as your risk tolerance, time frame in which you will need the money, and your needed rate of return based on income, expenses, life expectancy, and assets to name a few. My findings are supported by research. One such study is titled "Determinants of Financial Adequacy for Retirement" by Li, Montalto, and Geistfeld. Their research concluded that financial adequacy in retirement is contingent on how long one will live, consumption needs, financial resources, income sources, health, age of retirement, education, and marital status, among others. It is logical to conclude that our savings and investments have to fill the gap between our consumption (expenses) and our sources of income, such as pension and Social Security.

When one will need income and how much will be needed, along with risk tolerance, tells an advisor how to set up a portfolio. In other words, portfolio design is driven by your specific need—not the need of your neighbor, friend, relative, or well meaning Uncle Joe who wants to share with you his successful investment secrets. I am probably safe to say that your income, expenses, health, life expectancy, financial resources, and risk tolerance, are different than those you know, or those that you are related to—even Uncle Joe. Russ's father, like so many, unfortunately put his money in the same investment his friend used *without considering all implications. Not only did it cost him dearly, but the fallout troubles his son to this day.*

There is an old saying that you are probably familiar with and that is, "We don't plan to fail, we fail to plan." Only 11% of retirees enter retirement with a plan. Without a plan we are vulnerable to be tossed on the waves of uncertainty. We don't know our need, so we blindly follow the leadership of someone else who may be very well meaning, but has no basis in which to direct his investment recommendations. Following this course of action, we too may reap the whirlwind of making a decision vital to our financial well being without considering all implications.

Look at all implications before investing your hard earned money into anything. Your decision should be based on how the investment meets your specific needs. If you are getting your investment tips from your neighbor or Uncle Joe, take this to heart: *free advice may be the most expensive advice you ever receive.* Planning will help you to consider implications before you take action. Planning is the first step and following the plan is the next.

> *Planning is the first step and following the plan is the next.*

Behavior #8…*Thinking that errors made are more important than errors of omission.* Is losing $8,500 from a bad investment any different than losing $8,500 of annual purchasing power? Many people that I have met over the years seem to think so. How I draw that conclusion is, many people fear seeing a loss on their investment statement but do not put much thought into maintaining their purchasing power over time. Let's say that you started your retirement out with $500,000. You are healthy and relatively young and so it is reasonable to live another 19 years. The following graph shows the result of placing all of your savings in CDs and drawing money from them to supplement annual income needs. The illustration assumes a 4% pre-tax return and a 3% rate of inflation. *Your purchasing power is reduced by 43% over your life expectancy.*

Inflation and Purchasing Power

Widow Age 65
19 Year Life Expectancy
4% Certificate of Deposit Interest Rate
3% Inflation Rate
$500,000 Available for Investment
Never Uses Principal and Lives Off Interest

Year	Purchasing Power	CD Rate	Real Yield
Now	$500,000	4%	$20,000
10	$372,047	4%	$14,882
19	$285,143	4%	$11,406

43% Decrease in Purchasing Power over 19 Years

So ask yourself, is omitting the need and therefore the decision to invest in a way to help maintain your quality of life anymore costly then a loss in your portfolio? The affect on your comfort in retirement will probably be the same.

Behavior #9…*Putting All of Your Eggs in One Basket.* "Tis the part of a wise man to keep himself today for tomorrow, and not venture all his eggs in one basket." - Miguel de Cervantes, Don Quixote de la Mancha, 1605.

Contrary to Mr. Mancha, you may be familiar with the quote from Mark Twain, "Put all your eggs in the one basket and watch the basket." I believe there is wisdom in Mark Twain's quote when one owns a company that is providing her livelihood, but when it comes to investing, we are better served by following the advice of Mr. Mancha. Keeping our eggs in one basket and failing to diversify is asking for trouble. Why is that? Take for example investing money in a corporate bond. We are probably not involved in the day to day operation of the company that issued the bond. In other words, we are not running the operation—therefore, even though we watched the basket, we do not have much control over the performance of the basket, and as a result no influence over its value in the future. That being the case, we may need to buy bonds from a diverse number of companies to help guard against one company going out of business and leaving us holding a worthless piece of paper.

There should never be a moment during your lifetime when your life savings are not heavily diversified. Putting all of your eggs in one basket is asking for trouble. The

The Enron debacle is an example of the potentially disastrous results of not diversifying.

Enron debacle is an example of the potentially disastrous results of not diversifying.

Another misunderstanding, as it relates to diversification, is the act of holding a number of the same type of investments. Let's go back to the example of the corporate bond. You took the first step in diversifying. You bought bonds from several different companies—so far so good. Unfortunately, all you own is corporate bonds, and let's assume you bought them at about the same time and so they were paying about the same interest rate.

The second unfortunate problem is that they were all callable, and since interest rates declined, the companies called them so they could issue new bonds at lower rates. What you weren't counting on when you invested your money was a drop in interest rates and since you were living off of the interest, your standard of living suffered because you are now faced with buying bonds paying less interest. Even though you thought that you were diversifying by putting your money into a number of different bonds, you were not diversified by savings or investment type. This type of exposure is interest rate risk. You have nothing to protect yourself against interest rates dropping and therefore affecting your standard of living.

Lack of diversification by investment type also applies to stocks, bonds, and real estate, as well as other asset classes. This type of diversification is best remedied by the use of asset allocation as discussed earlier in this chapter.

PARTING WORDS REGARDING BEING A SMART INVESTOR

"Bulls make money and bears make money, but pigs get slaughtered." As this timeless old saying states, when stocks are providing us with great returns it's easy to get greedy. Stick with your plan and stay the course. What goes up will come down; it's not a question of "if" but "when." You're best served by heeding this historical fact of investing. An asset allocation model that fits your temperament as well as your time frame and is backed up by empirical data will help keep you from getting caught up in the frenzy.

Don't Let Fear Take You Off Course. Fear can be one of our greatest roadblocks to achieving financial security. Fear can keep

> *Fear can be one of our greatest roadblocks to achieving financial security.*

us from standing our ground and maintaining our courage in difficult times. Have you noticed that if we control our fear when faced with an aggressive dog that the dog usually loses much of its aggression? On the other hand, if we run from the dog his aggression will often times increase and we are then at risk of being chased. As difficult as it is, standing our ground and facing our fear may keep us from being bit.

While I may not have had much exposure to aggressive dogs (thank goodness), I can learn from someone else's experience. One of my favorite TV shows is the Dog Whisperer. Cesar Millan, the Dog Whisperer, is a cool customer when faced with unruly animals. He has learned from experience, and through understanding dog behavior, that remaining calm and assertive keeps him safe.

Although I do not have experience working with challenging dogs, I have had twenty years of experience working with financial planning issues. That experience tells me that when we run from our investment decisions, or we become fearful when faced with a financial crisis, we are at risk and we are vulnerable. If we are to be successful, we must map a destination, navigate the rough waters *THAT WILL HAPPEN*, and face down our fears standing our ground no matter how big the predator or the circumstances. If we apply the same principles to investing that Cesar applies to dog behavior, and remain calm and assertive in the face of fear, we too have a better chance of remaining safe.

SUMMARY

- As our life expectancy increases, so does our purchasing power risk. Although there is no guarantee that history will repeat itself, it is our best source for predictability. History tells us that by adding stocks to our portfolio we have a better chance of protecting our purchasing power over time.

- If you are uncomfortable with the risk that your portfolio requires, take the nine steps to reduce it that I laid out in this chapter.

- The wrong investor behavior will keep us from achieving our objectives and we become part of the herd.

- For nearly half a century, studies have shown that asset allocation, rather than individual security selection or market timing, is the most important determinant of total portfolio performance.

- By identifying short-term money, intermediate-term money, and long-term money, you can use the investment products that best match your time frame. Diversifying into different asset classes (such as equities, cash, fixed investments, real estate, and bonds) will help balance your portfolio and provide you with a smoother ride when a particular asset class is out of favor.

- Take a long-term approach to investing.
- Don't let fear take you off course. Plan to succeed and work your plan. Stick with it no matter what the media or your good friends say. If you are concerned about the quality and/or the appropriateness of your plan, get a second opinion. Doing nothing is not avoiding making a decision, it is a decision.

Chapter 2

Annuities …Why They Are Needed to Help Guard Against Longevity Risk

The Second Step to a Worry-Free Retirement

How to use the government and insurance company's money to help build your own financial security.

I live on a beautiful stretch of the Washougal River. One of my pleasures is feeding the wildlife. Most entertaining is the squirrel that makes frequent trips to the bird feeder bent on gathering all of the peanuts and leaving none. I started thinking about the instincts of squirrels and what they can teach us about money. While I could think of several applications, I limited them to the principles as they apply to longevity risk.

First, it was obvious the squirrel was not planning on eating his new found resources all at once. I believe it is safe to assume my friend would continue to store peanuts until no more were available. Actually, Alvin (I call him Alvin because as a kid I loved the show Alvin and the Chipmunks. I realize Alvin is a squirrel and not a chipmunk but what are you going to do…I'm sure he would appreciate the celebrity) would be happy if he could store so many nuts that no matter how long he lived he would never run out. I also thought how his security would be lessened if there was such a thing as a peanut collector; for every 5 peanuts that Alvin worked so hard to secure, he had to give one to the peanut collector. If only Alvin could figure out a way to cut the peanut collector out of the picture (don't worry this doesn't get violent) while storing food for a long and uncertain season.

What if Alvin could invest his peanuts so that they could make more for him? Also, what if he worked it out that he did not have to pay the peanut collector, so therefore the peanuts that normally went to the collector, Alvin could use to build up his own peanut portfolio? When Alvin was ready to kick back and retire from peanut gathering, what if he could trade some of his savings for a stream of peanuts that he could never outlive, while the balance of his portfolio could be invested in such a way as to continue to keep his portfolio away from the peanut collector? Also, what if Alvin needed long-term care and couldn't afford insurance, nor could he qualify due to health problems, but he could still get the care he needed and keep his peanuts? I believe other squirrels would be lining up to learn Alvin's secret.

You may be saying to yourself, "David, I think this a cute little squirrel story too, but what does all of this have to do with annuities and the role they play in protecting retirees from longevity risk?" My answer is—plenty. No matter what you or I think of insurance companies, annuities are the answer to Alvin's longevity problem as well as ours.

While over the years annuities have received some negative press—and I have agreed with some of those findings as it applies to old-style annuities—thanks to modern innovations, many retirement specialists like myself have started to embrace them. As we move forward into a new era, contemporary annuities will play a key role in helping protect us from outliving our financial resources. They will be uniquely positioned to help guard us against three areas of vulnerability. These three areas are:

1. Protecting assets from the cost of long-term care.
2. Protection against outliving our income.
3. Reduction of taxation during accumulation and when we take income.

Those over age 50 own more than 60% of all annuities.[4] Many retirees own more than one annuity. The reason is, most people want to keep their money protected from the tax man. Astute people know that every tax dollar paid unnecessarily to the IRS slowly erodes financial security. Although annuities have helped in this regard, from my experience, annuities are not used

> *As we move forward into a new era, contemporary annuities will play a key role in helping protect us from outliving our financial resources.*

to their full capabilities. In order to use all the tools at our disposal, financial professionals as well as the public, need to be made aware of how annuities will play a key role in protecting us from impoverishment.

In this chapter I will start out by giving you an overview of annuities, what they are, the popular types, and how they are taxed. Once you have a basic understanding, I will then present the facts on why annuities will play an important role in helping us protect against longevity risk. From there I will address the most common negative attacks on annuities and why they are either no longer correct or irrelevant. Then I will share with you some important advice if you own or are thinking about purchasing an annuity. Last, I will summarize key information that will help you. So let's get started!

ANNUITY BASICS AND HOW THEY ARE TAXED

An annuity is a written contract between an insurance company, an owner, and an annuitant. Many times the owner and annuitant is the same person. The contract is unilateral, meaning that the insurance company cannot break the contract while the owner can. Under the agreement, the owner and not the annuitant, if different people, has all rights. As shown in Figure 3, while money is in the annuity, under Internal Revenue Code (IRC) section 72(c), it is not taxable or in other words is tax deferred similar to money in a retirement account. The concept is simple; if we can get a loan from the government by way of deferring taxes, then we can use the government's money to compound in our own account. Money that was leaking through our fingertips is now captured and used for our benefit. *This is one reason pension plans, IRAs, and annuities are so popular because they function by way of the same concept.*

When putting money in the annuity you have the option of choosing between a one-time lump sum or use what is called a flexible premium annuity which allows on-going contributions. When taking money out, the owner has the option of taking it one of two ways, either random withdrawals

> *Under Internal Revenue Code (IRC) section 72(c), annuities are tax deferred similar to money in a retirement account.*

or tax favored income. Another term for tax favored income is annuitization. When one annuitizes the contract he or she is exchanging the money in the annuity for a stream of income. I will cover a little later in this chapter how you can receive tax favored income by annuitizing and why a once rarely used option is now a friend when it comes to protecting against impoverishment.

While you can reach in and take money out of an annuity at any time, a penalty may be assessed if you do so during the surrender charge period. Most companies provide a liquidity feature and allow you to take 10% of the total amount in the annuity as a withdrawal during a contract year without penalty. To give an additional layer of security, some companies provide a feature called principal guarantee. Principal guarantee means that you will never get back less then what you put into the annuity minus withdrawals. So for example, if you decided to take out all of your money during the surrender charge period, the penalty cannot dip into your principal. The worst case scenario is that you may lose the accrued interest.

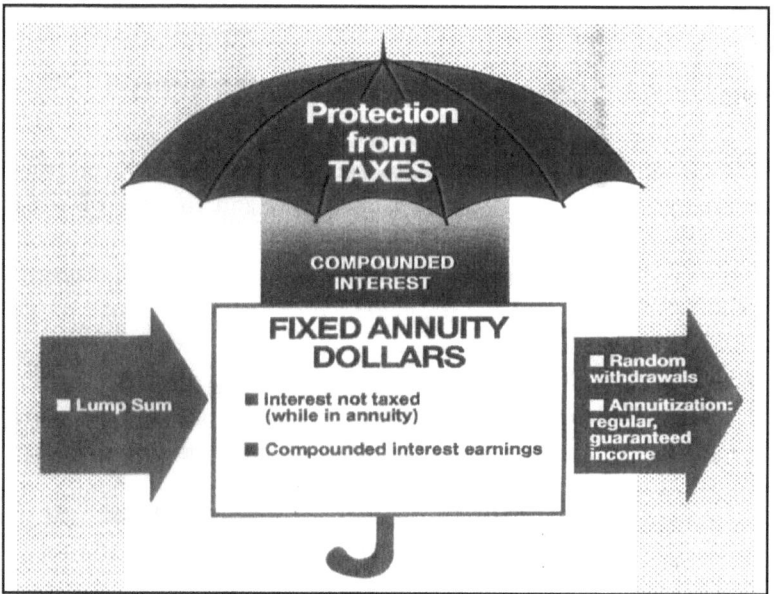

Figure 3

Originally designed to provide retirement income, most people use annuities for the tax deferral benefit. Retirees have caught on to this opportunity and many use annuities to cut taxes. Rarely in the past have annuity owners taken money out. Most pass away without ever touching the money. This supports one of the main objections to annuities—which I address later in this chapter—and that is the fact that the annuity does not receive a step-up in tax basis at the death of the owner and or annuitant. If you are not familiar with the term *step-up in basis*, I will cover it later in this chapter.

As I mentioned, annuities benefit from tax deferred compounding like retirement plans such as a 401(k), 403(b), or an IRA, etc. Graph 5 shows the power of tax deferral. In this example a person in a 28% tax bracket sets aside $100,000 for 15 years and receives an 8% return. You can see the difference if one pays taxes on the interest every year compared to using the government's money to help build a bigger pot of capital. I don't know about you, but when it comes to financial security, I'll take the bigger pot of money.

> *After we grow a bigger pot of money, we are at risk of returning some of it if we don't understand how to use the annuity to create tax efficient income.*

Remember I said earlier that annuities are not used to their full potential. Why? Because after we grow a bigger pot of money, we are at risk of returning some of it if we don't understand how to use the annuity to create tax efficient income.

BENEFIT FROM TAX DEFERRED GROWTH

- Tax-deferred compounding
- Over time, more actual dollars

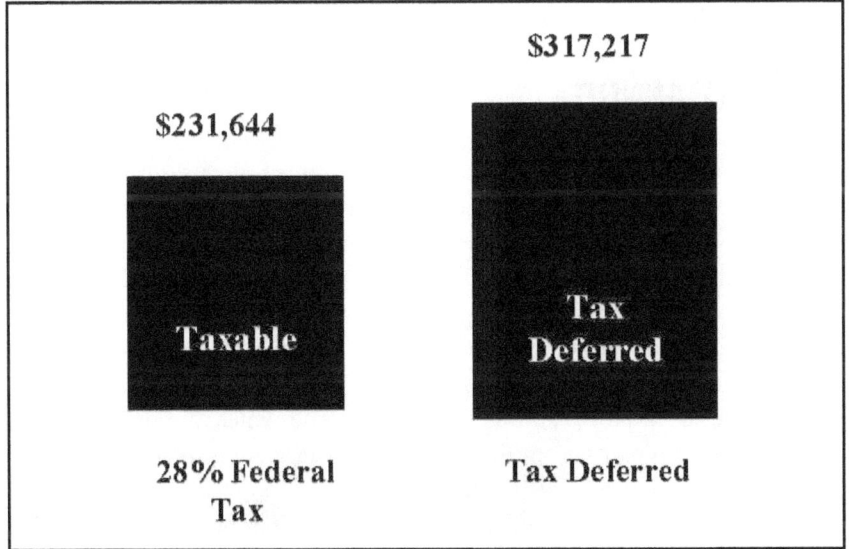

$231,644 — Taxable — 28% Federal Tax

$317,217 — Tax Deferred — Tax Deferred

Graph 5

If there is a need, an insurance company will fill it and annuities are no exception. Depending on age, need, and risk tolerance, the market will let you choose between a fixed, variable, index, and a single premium immediate annuity.

FIXED ANNUITY

With a fixed annuity, an insurance company pays a fixed rate of return for a specified period of time. The rate can be fixed for the term of the annuity or it can change each contract year. If you are curious about when the contract year started, you can call the agent, the company, or check the policy. Fixed annuities are the choice of most retirees since it is similar to a Certificate of deposit (CD). Like a CD, an annuity pays a fixed interest rate for a period of

> *Fixed annuities are the choice of most retirees since it is similar to a Certificate of deposit (CD).*

time and penalties are assessed if taken out early. While a CD is issued by the bank, and is therefore FDIC insured (if too much money is not put in the CD), the annuity is issued by an insurance company. While insurance companies have safety nets to help protect the public against insolvency, such as legal reserves and the State Guarantee Association, it is still important to find out the financial ratings of the insurance company.

VARIABLE ANNUITY

While many variable annuities have fixed sub accounts similar to a fixed annuity, most people use variable annuities for the variable sub accounts. Sub accounts inside a variable annuity are simply mutual fund type investments that are not subject to tax—in other words they are tax deferred. Many of the top fund managers are hired by the insurance companies to manage these sub accounts.

Although variable annuities and mutual funds share some similarities, they are different when it comes to how they are taxed. Unlike mutual funds whereby the tax is passed through to the customer when the manager buys and/or sells securities, or when the customer sells and moves to another mutual fund, those that own variable annuities are allowed to defer the tax as long as the money remains in the annuity—again the bigger pot of money theory. You could say it is like investing in mutual funds with a tax deferred benefit.

A proliferation of investment options has occurred in recent years along with many new features. Some companies have made available index funds (not to be mistaken for an Index Annuity) that do not require active management which can drive down the cost for the investor.

Unlike a fixed annuity where the insurance company is responsible to guarantee the payment to the annuity owner, in the case of a variable annuity, the money held in the sub accounts are separate and not at risk if the insurance company becomes insolvent.

Variable annuities pass the investment return on to the owner. Therefore the investment risk also belongs to the owner. Because many in retirement are risk adverse, and justifiably so, the companies have added an insurance feature to variable annuities. The feature is called a death benefit. How the death benefit works is, if the annuity owner should die and the value of the sub accounts are less than he or she invested (less any withdrawals) the insurance company is under contract to make up the difference. So let's say an individual purchased an annuity and the market was down when the person passed away; the heirs have some protection and are made whole. This benefit is not free. Companies charge what is called an M&E (Mortality and Expense) fee which varies between companies. You can also purchase additional guarantees for an additional fee. Some of the more popular are:

- A step-up in the death benefit. So if you were to take a step-up option that compounded annually at 5%, and your investments only returned 3% and you passed away, your family would receive the 5% compounded accumulation amount.

- A rider that guarantees a specified return no matter what the market does when you get ready to start taking income.

INDEX ANNUITY

Index annuities are relatively new. While fixed and variable annuities were popularized in the 1970s, index annuities came on the scene in 1995. Index annuities are kind of a hybrid of fixed and variable annuities. Index annuities share some of the same features. Where the fixed annuity provides a specified rate of return and the variable annuity allows for a return with no ceiling and no safety net should the market drop, the index annuity meets somewhere in the middle. The index annuity earns a minimum rate of interest and offers the potential for excess interest based on the performance of an index such as the S&P 500. Unlike the variable annuity whereby you can lose money if the market goes down, the index annuity is protected from market risk. In other words, you can never lose money no matter what the market does. An owner does not share in the market loss, nor does he or she receive all of the market gain.

With an index annuity the owner will participate in the gain up to a cap or what is called a participation rate. The caps and participation rates can vary from annuity to annuity and company to company. Based on a participation formula, the owner receives interest credited to his account annually. Once the interest is credited to the owner *it can never be lost*, even if the market subsequently declines. How the interest is credited also varies from company to company. Jack Marrion, a recognized expert, stated in his book *Index Annuities Power and Protection*, "I've done enough analysis to see that all of these other crediting methods should produce about the same results if you wait long enough—unless you know for certain how the stock market will move in the future—so the key is picking an index annuity carrier that will treat you well down the road."

Those that purchase index annuities typically do not have the temperament for the stock market, but want the opportunity for a greater return then a bank product or fixed annuity can give them. As I covered in Chapter 1, if held long enough, participation in the stock market gives one the greatest opportunity for gain, but for those that want a guarantee and are satisfied with less than the overall market return—in my opinion—an index annuity is a good option.

SINGLE PREMIUM IMMEDIATE ANNUITY

All annuities have an income feature that allows either what is called a systematic withdrawal or annuitization. The difference is with most companies you can take a systematic withdrawal either occasionally or continually, whatever your particular need is at the time. Keep in mind if you are still in the surrender charge period, if you take in excess of what the company allows—which is usually 10%—you may be subject to a penalty. Be aware that if you choose to annuitize, some of the old-style policies, will not allow you to change your decision once you make it. When an owner annuitizes the contract, he or she is exchanging the money in the annuity for a stream of income. Choices range from lifetime income that cannot be outlived, or a specified period of time with many options in between. While annuitization has been rarely used, it is becoming more prominent due to longevity risk. I will explain why later in this chapter.

A Single Premium Immediate Annuity is simply putting money in an annuity and immediately receiving income. Unlike annuities that grow tax deferred, the immediate annuity skips the deferral stage and goes directly into the payout stage. If you have received a pension from a company, it works much the same. Most pensions generally allow you to choose between a life only payout or a joint and survivor payout, but rarely a period certain.

TAXATION OF ANNUITIES

While annuities grow tax deferred during the accumulation stage, they are taxed when money comes out. If you reach in and take money out, you are taxed on the interest first. For example, you put $50,000 into an annuity, it has grown to $60,000, and you want to take a withdrawal. The first $10,000—the deferred gain—is taxed as ordinary income. If you dip into the $50,000 it is *not* taxed since it is considered a return of principal. In the case of annuitization, taxation is treated differently. In the example above, once a payout period is chosen, let's say 5 years; the $60,000 would be paid out plus interest over the time period. The IRS considers the payment interest plus a return of principal and they allow an exclusion ratio similar to selling real estate on a contract. Each payment received consists of part principal and part interest. So let's say that the overall return paid is $60,000 and the initial investment is $50,000; the formula is $50,000 divided by $60,000 or 83% (rounded for simplicity). For every payment received, 83% of it is not taxable. Why is this important? It provides us an opportunity to receive income, tax efficiently.

WHO PAYS THE TAX AT DEATH?

Historically, very few annuity owners annuitize their contract—most use annuities for tax deferral. That being the case, at death, many annuity owners pass the annuity on to the next generation. Usually annuity owners are surprised to learn, when they die, their beneficiaries will have to pay the tax on the deferred gain. This can be disconcerting to the family because many times the annuity owner's children are in a higher tax bracket. Over the years, I have discovered that most people who own annuities do not understand who ultimately pays the tax on the gain when they die. Most think annuities are treated like stocks where no tax is passed

> *Usually annuity owners are surprised to learn, when they die, their beneficiaries will have to pay the tax on the deferred gain.*

on to the next generation. Once informed that taxes *are* passed on, many become understandably concerned. (I do have to say that I have met with a few people over the years that are not on the best terms with their children, nevertheless most would rather see their money go to family rather than the IRS.)

While the use of annuities is an excellent way to accumulate money over time, they are not a good transfer vehicle to pass to heirs. If one wants to transfer money to the next generation after death, there are better more efficient ways to go about it.

THE IMPORTANT ROLE OF ANNUITIES IN HELPING TO PROVIDE SECURITY

PROTECTING ASSETS FROM THE COST OF LONG-TERM CARE

Annuities issued by insurance companies (as opposed to private annuities), are not only an important financial product that can protect the assets of a husband and wife when one of them needs long-term care…*it is the only financial product that the government accepts as a vehicle to guard against having to spend-down assets in order to qualify for Medicaid.* I show you in greater detail how a Medicaid annuity provides protection in Chapter 4, which addresses long-term care. For now, know this; *if used correctly,* an annuity will help protect the healthy spouse from becoming impoverished. It can be the bridge between financial security for the healthy spouse and asset depletion. Be forewarned, if used incorrectly for Medicaid planning purposes, it can do more damage than good.

> *An annuity is the only financial product that the government accepts as a vehicle to guard against having to spend-down assets in order to qualify for Medicaid.*

Many people that I have worked with over the years ask me the same question, "How long will my money last if I have to pay the cost of long-term care for my spouse and also have to pay my bills?" The thing that is so sad about this predicament is many people run out of money when they do not have to. This fact greatly upsets me because in most cases, *it just flat doesn't have to happen* no matter what so called "experts" say. Give me a break isn't caring for a loved one with health problems stressful enough without worrying about going broke?

Some professionals thought that Medicaid annuities, as an asset protection strategy, would be wiped out by the government with the creation of the Deficit Reduction Act of 2005 (DRA 2005). While the government did put some restrictions on the use of annuities, they are alive and well when using them for the protection of the healthy spouse.

The use of annuities will be key for many facing long-term care that do not have, nor can they qualify, for long-term care insurance. For those of you who have loved ones faced with needing long-term care and are worried about if you will be able to pay the bills, Chapter 4 can provide you with a life line. Since I cover the use of Medicaid annuities in Chapter 4, for now I will leave it at this, *many of our older population cannot qualify for, nor can they afford, a long- term care insurance policy. As compassionate caring people, we cannot throw them out in the cold.* Some are now faced with needing long-term care and the spouse does not know if he or she can pay the bills. A Medicaid annuity can help give the healthy spouse peace of mind. I believe it is important that those that are concerned about paying for long-term care should know about the annuity as an asset protection tool.

PROTECTION AGAINST OUTLIVING OUR INCOME

Various studies are emerging promoting the use of annuities to guard against longevity risk. Why is that? In the past retirees received two sources of guaranteed income—company pension plans called defined benefit (DB) plans—and Social Security. In a little over twenty years, DB plans have decreased from 175,000 to just about 25,000. During the same time period, 401(k) defined contribution plans (DC) have increased in number from 17,000 to over 450,000.[7] The shift by companies away from defined benefit plans is continuing to increase. Employers have switched from providing income to retirees, to putting the burden on those in retirement to make their *own* money last a lifetime. Also concerning is the fact that Social Security will pay less in benefits, to those retiring now and in the future, then it did for their parents.

What does the reduction in DB plans and Social Security benefits mean to retirees?—less guaranteed income to pay for needs. We can no longer say "I was loyal to the company and now they will in turn take care of me." It is up to us to make our own money last and the stakes are high. If we are not successful, we can no longer look to the company that employed us, but instead we must look to ourselves.

> *What does the reduction in DB plans and Social Security benefits mean to retirees?— less guaranteed income to pay for needs.*

Many financial professionals believe that those who want to maintain their standard of living in retirement will need to replace 70-80 percent of the income that they made during their working years. From my experience, I think 70-80 percent is low and here is why. Due to modern technology, medical breakthroughs, and healthier lifestyles; we tend to be more active at retirement age then our parents were. During the first several years many travel and are on the go. Because of increased activity, dialing down spending does not usually happen. But as we age, most of us slow down a little more which starts to curtail spending. That being said, I believe many retirees will be in for a rude financial awakening if they underestimate their spending needs in retirement especially since 78% of retirees do not have a financial plan.

So, what we have is the demise of guaranteed income from companies in the form of DB plans, greater activity in retirement leading to more spending, and we are living longer. Add to that, there will be a smaller population of workers asked to provide the largest number of people entering retirement in history with Social Security income benefits. What that means is, not only are Social Security benefits dropping, but also the system is currently unfunded which should tell us that depending on Social Security for a portion of our retirement income is shaky at best.

What is the answer? We need our own defined benefit plan—a plan we cannot outlive—a guaranteed flow of lifetime income. How do we do it? By using a life annuity; *a life annuity can provide more income for a longer period of time then other savings or investment options.* In addition, a life income annuity provides a higher rate of return than one can get on a similar, but unannuitized portolio.[9] Annuitants (those receiving the income) benefit from what is called "mortality premium" which equates to an additional rate of return. By design, an annuity can provide us with our own inexhaustible pension for as many years as we are on this earth—the end result—more security that we cannot outlive.

Many financial experts have come to the conclusion that a life annuity adds the greatest security to retirees; some of the most prominent in the world being Noble Prize winners. Studies supporting this conclusion have been conducted at MIT, The Wharton School, Berkley, Yale, Harvard, London Business School, Hebrew University, Carnegie Mellon, and others.[7]

Although it may be tempting, I caution you not to go out and buy a life annuity. If you do it wrong you may not be able to fix it. An incorrect purchase of a life annuity can chip away at your standard of living in later years. Do some planning and make sure that what you are doing—or plan on doing—is right for you.

REDUCTION OF TAXATION DURING ACCUMULATION AND WHEN TAKING INCOME

> *Many financial experts have come to the conclusion that a life annuity adds the greatest security to retirees.*

It is not what you make but what you keep that matters. *Too many seniors give back a portion of their income to the government simply because they did not know there might be a better way.* Judge Learned Hand's remark that there are two tax systems in the United States, one for the informed and one for the uninformed, is well known to many. A judge on the Second Circuit Court of Appeals, Hand (1872 – 1961) is often quoted for his view that there is nothing sinister in arranging one's affairs to keep taxes as low as possible.

The government makes it easy to pay taxes while making it more complicated to reduce or eliminate taxes. Complicated or not, we have a right to reduce our tax burden under the rules of our system. The one catch is…*you have to know how to go about it in order to do it.* What you don't know *can* hurt you. Being an informed tax payer puts us more in control and helps us keep more of our money.

If used correctly, annuities are an uncomplicated tool that can help us save tax dollars. As a sole provider of annuities, insurance companies are uniquely positioned to help us build a bigger pot of

> *Judge Learned Hand's remarked that there are two tax systems in the United States, one for the informed and one for the uninformed.*

money by keeping capital gains, dividends, and interest, from being taxed while growing. And if we know how to go about it—annuities can also provide us with tax efficient income at the time we need it. The result is more money to help keep us financially independent. Here is an example.

THE SNEAKY TAX

Let me ask you, if you were walking along the street and someone threw a $1 bill out of their car window, would you stop and pick it up? I know I would and I think you would too. If the government sent you a check for $2000 every year, would you take one half of it and give it back…even if you weren't required to? I think you would probably say, "Are you crazy? Of course I wouldn't." Well neither would I, but the fact of the matter is, many do. I have met with retirees over the years that without knowing it, were giving part of their income back to the government. When I asked them if that was what they wanted to do, they gave me a response that implied they thought that I must be loony. The problem was, *no one informed them, not even their tax person,* that they were volunteering to give back part of their income to the government. No one told Trudy either! This is her story.

TRUDY'S TAXING EXPERIENCE

Trudy is one of the nicest people that I have ever had the pleasure to help—a character that loves to laugh and enjoys getting a chuckle out of those that have the pleasure to be in her company. We hit it off at our first meeting because I also love to joke and have a good laugh. An infectious person,

Trudy enjoyed life and her house was adorned by pictures of those that have shared it with her. She had been blessed by a loving marriage that lasted 55 years. Her husband had passed away a few years prior to our meeting, and though still heartbroken, she was determined to continue to live a full life. A fun and funny woman that was seldom serious about much of anything, Trudy was concerned about paying more than her fair share of taxes.

Trudy looked at me and said, "Do you see any way that I can save taxes? I am proud to live in this country, it has been good to me and my family, but if I am allowed to save taxes, why not?" After reviewing Trudy's finances along with her tax returns, I told Trudy that she was paying more in taxes than required. I said, "You, like many others that I have worked with over the years, have been bit by the *sneaky tax*." Trudy said, "What in the heck is the *sneaky tax*?" I responded, "You are paying taxes on your Social Security income." "I am paying taxes on my Social Security? Isn't that like paying taxes on my taxes?" Trudy said with a look of irritation on her face. "Well put, I said. You and your husband paid your FICA taxes during your working years, and now you are paying taxes on those taxes," I confirmed. Trudy asked, "Can we do anything about it?" "Yes", I said.

I will share with you what Trudy did to eliminate the tax on her benefits in just a moment, but first I think you need to read this which will shine a light on why I call it the *sneaky tax*.

This is off of the Social Security website at http://www.socialsecurity.gov/planners/taxes.htm   "Some people have to pay federal income taxes on their Social Security benefits. This usually happens *only* if you have other *substantial* income (such as wages, self-employment, interest, dividends and *other taxable income* that must be reported on your tax return) in addition to your benefits." (Italics added.)

Reading this statement, a retiree might think their Social Security will never be taxed because:

1. They do not believe their income is substantial.
2. The Social Security website specifically says, "Interest, dividends, and other taxable income."

Many retirees who own tax-free bonds are confident the statement above does not apply to them, and understandably so, because tax-free bonds are not associated with *taxable* income.

First, let's look at substantial income. If a single person has income of $25,000 to $34,000 the lesser of one-half of excess income or one-half of Social Security benefits may be taxable. Over $34,000, the percent of taxation increases to 85%. A married couple may be taxed at 50% of benefits with income of $32,000 and increasing to 85% at $44,000. Are you kidding me? In this day and age, a single person with $25,000 of income or a married couple with income of $32,000 qualifies as substantial income? Give me a break!

Next let's look at "interest, dividends, and other taxable income." Many people I have met with over the years purchase municipal bonds in order to keep from paying taxes. I think for those trying to reduce taxes who are needing income, purchasing tax-free bonds makes sense. The problem lies in the fact that many people put money in tax-free bonds as a holding place, thinking that since they do not need income from the bonds, they will simply reinvest it by buying more bonds. Here is the *sneaky tax* part; to the surprise of many, *the interest from tax-free bonds — even though it is not being used for income—still gets counted as income to determine if Social Security benefits are taxed.* Yes, that is true, tax-free income, under Social Security interpretations becomes taxable income (which in this case sounds like an oxymoron). Interesting, wouldn't you say? Be careful, you can make your head sore by scratching it. See what I mean by having to be informed? With all due respect to retirees, who researches this stuff? (I do, but that is my job.) The problem is, unless you are *informed*, one pays the tax not knowing there may be a way to reduce or even eliminate it. Let's get back to Trudy so I can show you how we *eliminated* this tax.

> *The interest from tax free bonds—even though it is not being used for income— still gets counted as income to determine if Social Security benefits are taxed.*

First thing I looked at was her short and long-term income needs adjusted for inflation. Confirming the fact that she *did not currently need income from the money held in the bonds*, we moved the money to a tax deferred annuity. Why? Unlike tax-free bonds, the money in a tax deferred vehicle (like an annuity) is not counted when determining if Social Security income is taxed. A 1099 is not sent to the tax payer or the IRS, so the government has no record of it.

Some might think, "Wait a minute, you're telling me that you took a tax-free investment and moved it to a tax deferred investment. Doesn't that mean Trudy will have to pay tax on this money down the road? The answer is… *maybe…,*BUT remember, it is not what you make—but what you keep that matters. By using the annuity, based on projections, she will have a bigger pot of money to pay taxes with and she will end up with more money even after the taxes are paid. Here is why.

When we look historically at the performance of bonds compared to stocks, we see that stocks give us the best opportunity to accumulate money over time. Therefore, I put together an asset allocation model designed for growth inside Trudy's annuity. Since Trudy did not need the income from this money for several years, we eliminated the tax on her Social Security benefits, and added that money to her annuity. Each year Trudy is able to take the taxes she saves, and invest it in her new portfolio. The end result is more accumulated money over time. Trudy is better off over the long-term. Happy to put the money *she has been giving to the government* back in her own pocket, Trudy had peace of mind knowing that money will now be growing on her behalf and will be available for her needs in the future. She was able to keep more of what she made. It is too bad she didn't know about this sooner.

If you are interested in gathering more information regarding taxation on Social Security benefits you can do so by reviewing IRS publication 915.

Trudy's story is one example of how annuities can help save taxes. By reducing taxation during accumulation and while receiving income, annuities help us keep more of our own money. As an informed citizen, we can invest in such a way that the money that normally goes to the government stays in our account and works for us. The result is more money and that equals greater financial security.

NEGATIVE COMMENTS REGARDING ANNUITIES AND WHY THEY ARE EITHER NO LONGER CORRECT OR NOT RELEVANT

After our fourth meeting together, Stan and Rita were at the point of implementing their plan. As with all clients, I charged a fee to shepherd them through the planning process and once it is at the final stage, they have the option to implement the plan with anyone that they feel can do the job. In this case as it is in most cases, they asked me to help them with the implementation process.

Stan asked, "What investments do you recommend for our non-IRA long-term money?" I said, "We have three primary options. (see Graph 6)

| | *Tax* | *Tax* |
| *Taxable* | *Managed* | *Deferred* |

Graph 6

"We can choose taxable investments, tax managed accounts, or we can use tax deferred investments such as annuities." (I did not bring up tax-free investments such as municipal bonds, because for long-term money, over time, tax-free bonds would increase the chance of eroding their purchasing power.) When the discussion of annuities came up, I could see an immediate change in Rita's body language. I asked, "Rita, is everything okay?" She replied, "I know we told you that we want to reduce our taxes but I have read things about annuities that cause me some concern." "Fair enough", I said, "Do you mind sharing your concerns with me?" Rita went on to say, "I understand that annuities can create a tax problem for our children when we pass away, and when we take money out they are taxed at a higher rate than mutual funds. Also, they have very high fees which reduce the return and both Stan and I do not want to pay higher fees."

Rita had reason to be concerned. Who wouldn't, unless you have the whole story? Many articles regarding annuities do not present the entire picture. In all fairness to those that write much of the negatives, they are going off the following: in the past, few people have taken income from annuities and most owners have passed them on to heirs. Also, old-style annuity fees have been high. That being the case, their concerns are founded.

I said to Rita, "You and Stan have done a good job of accumulating money for retirement. About 60% of your money is in your retirement plans. I think you would agree that your retirement plans have served you well." Rita replied, "Yes I am glad that we had them available to help us save." "Let me ask you this, why did you put most of your money in your retirement plans instead of just investing outside of them?" Rita responded, "Well, we were able to put money in and our employers added to it every month. We also received a tax deduction. Also, our money grew without us having to pay taxes each year." "If you wouldn't have received a tax deduction and the company didn't add to it, do you think, as a savings option, it would have still been an attractive alternative to paying tax on the growth each year?" I asked. "I guess so," she said. I responded, "So, if the only alternative was to pay tax on the gain every year, the tax deferred option would have been more appealing to you?" "I certainly think it would have been the smarter choice," she replied.

"One last question, would you have been discouraged from using retirement accounts knowing that your heirs would pay tax on

> *Old-style annuities have received negative press and some negatives were founded.*

money left in the retirement account after both of you have passed away?" Rita responded with a no. She continued, "I think whatever the children receive is more than they have now. The money is really for our security. Of course I would like to cut out the tax man if possible. But I have read enough to know that with IRAs and retirement accounts, the children can stretch out the taxes over their lifetime. I understand annuities do not allow beneficiaries to stretch out the taxes, so our children would have to pay the tax immediately, which could be costly for them."

The concerns that Rita raised were three of the four main objections to using annuities. The four are:

1. At the death of the owner an annuity does not get a step-up in tax basis while stocks do.

2. Annuities, unlike stocks or mutual funds that own stocks, are taxed at ordinary income rates while stocks are taxed at lower capital gains rates.

3. The fees are too high.

4. They have surrender charges, and therefore you are locking up your money.

I will cover each objection one at a time like I did with Stan and Rita.

Objection #1…*At the death of the owner an annuity does not get a step-up in tax basis which equates to the heirs paying more in taxes.* Rita was correct. Annuities do not receive a step-up in tax basis when the money passes to the heirs. Remember, the spouse is the only one that can continue the contract without having to pay the deferred tax. Here is how the step-up in basis works. Let's say your parents want to pass the stocks they own to you at their death and they paid $5.00 a share for the stock. At their passing the stock is worth $10.00. If the stock is passed to you through their estate (by will or trust), you will receive it at a tax basis of $10.00 a share. What this means to you is, if you turn around and sell it you will only pay tax on the gain over $10.00. In addition, you will be taxed at the lower capital gains rates.

In the example above, the stocks would receive a step-up in basis *only* if they were passed outside of a qualified plan such as a 401(k), or outside of an IRA. Here is the point, if they are passed inside of a qualified plan or an IRA, they would not receive the step-up in basis. So think about this, does the fact that qualified money does not receive a step-up in basis make qualified plans less popular with the public? Rita didn't think so. Next, let's take IRAs. Because they do not receive a step-up in basis, do people quit putting money in them? Still...*no*. How about non-deductible IRAs, where the only benefit to the owner is tax deferral? Also... *no*. Why is that? Because with all qualified money and IRAs, they provide us with the power of tax deferral. Remember when I said it is a good thing if we can get a loan from the government and we can use the government's money to provide us with tax deferred compounding. That is what qualified plans and IRAs do for us. And guess what? So do annuities. That is why so many people like them. The bottom line is *given the option of investing money in a taxable, as opposed to a tax favored investment, people choose tax favored.*

Remember, Rita had commented that the government allows the beneficiary to *stretch* the taxes on IRAs over the life expectancy of the beneficiary. Rita was under the impression that annuities did not provide the same stretch benefit. Rita had been misinformed. Thanks to some innovative insurance companies, you can now stretch a non-qualified annuity (a non IRA or qualified annuity) over the life of the beneficiary just like with an IRA.

I think it is important to make the point here that by proper planning and utilizing the annuity correctly, less of an issue would be created when it comes to the step-up in basis. Annuities, like IRAs and qualified money, are great tools for accumulating money but are not designed to transfer to the next generation with any great efficiency. I know from experience that if more people would have a financial plan completed, they would have a good idea of what money will be consumed during their life time and what money will transfer to the next generation. Knowing what money will be consumed,

> *Given the option of investing money in a taxable, as opposed to a tax favored investment, people choose tax favored.*

and what money will probably transfer, allows for the use of proper products and investments designed to benefit the owner as well as the next generation.

The full power of the annuity can be brought into play. With proper planning the retirees will receive tax efficient savings and so will the heirs.

My question to those who are critical of annuities is; given the opportunity would you fund an IRA or a qualified plan? I believe most would say yes. That being said, my advice to them is not to rule out annuities for money exposed to taxes.

Objection #2...*Annuities, unlike stocks or mutual funds, are taxed at ordinary income rates, while mutual funds and stocks are taxed at lower capital gains rates.* This is true to some extent but this is just part of the story. If you are taking income from an annuity, and you are being taxed at ordinary rates, you are probably paying more taxes than you have to. A tax benefit that annuities provide and is seldom written about, and seldom used when taking income, is annuitization. Remember that when one opts to annuitize, the insurance company sends payments which consist of part interest and part principal until the principal is paid back to the customer. Typically, only a small part of the income received is taxable because the principal portion is tax-free. As I pointed out, and I think it bears repeating, if you sold a property that had a lot of deferred gain, would you typically sell it and pay all of the tax in one year? With our graduated tax rates, in most situations, it is better to spread the gain out over several years, given a competitive interest rate. Annuitization works on the same principle.

The problem lies in the fact that only a small percentage of annuity owners ever annuitize their policies. What that means is that when most people ask for income from their annuity, they take a withdrawal, or what is also called systematic income. When they take systematic income, interest is paid out first, which is taxed at ordinary income rates. In the case of Stan and Rita, their financial plan showed that

> *If you are taking income from an annuity, and you are being taxed at ordinary rates, you are probably paying more taxes than you have to.*

they will probably consume the money in question during their lifetime. The plan is, when money is needed, to annuitize in order to take advantage of the exclusion ratio (receiving part principal and part interest each payment). So in their case, as with my other client's that own annuities, the ordinary income tax objection is mitigated.

I have to admit, years ago I was not a proponent of annuitization. I felt strongly that too much control was given up and that inflation would erode purchasing power years down the road. I have since changed my mind for the following reasons:

1. Annuitization provides the retiree with tax efficient income.

2. Taxation on Social Security benefits can often be reduced and sometimes eliminated without affecting income and lifestyle. Income tax savings will play a key role in helping to keep us from running out of money.

3. Recent studies support the fact that by using a life annuity (which is annuitized income) *it is possible to completely eliminate longevity risk.*[8]

Using annuities to build wealth through tax deferral and then distribute income by way of annuitization eliminates the ordinary income and capital gains objection.

Objection #3… *The fees are too high.* For those not current on annuities, what I am about to say may shock them. *High fees are voluntary.* I know some will say no way, but what I am telling you is a fact. Now here is the problem and what I believe is the *main reason* why annuities get a bad rap. Annuities are too often sold instead of using them as a means to meet a need or solve a financial problem. Here is what I mean; let's say a person contacts you and wants to sell you an annuity. She represents XYZ insurance company and she is feeling the pressure to meet her sales quota. She starts talking about all the great things an annuity can do for you. Her pitch is convincing, and before you know it you have invested your money in the annuity, not knowing that you bought the company's Cadillac when you only needed a Chevy. Or possibly you didn't need an annuity at all. Well, anyway, you bought the annuity and the sales rep walks away with the highest commission possible.

> *Recent studies support the fact that by using a life annuity (which is annuitized income) it is possible to completely eliminate longevity risk.*

Because of salespeople taking advantage of the public, advisors who want to do a good job for their clients are up against the negative press. Good and ethical advisors, as well as annuity providers, get bad mouthed for recommending annuities because of the unethical practices of others. Because of that, the ones who suffer the most are the consumers since the whole story is not told. From my experience, when any savings or investment vehicle is used to meet a specific need—be it an annuity, mutual fund, money market, etc.—and after a thorough analysis it is the investment or savings option that best fits the need or solves the problem, *then and only then should it be recommended.* With this approach the need is determined, and if an annuity makes sense, the client decides the bells and whistles that give them the most peace of mind, and the fees are a result of that decision. Nothing more—nothing less—*pure and simple.*

So what are these fees that get the most press? First, I will tackle *management fees.* Yes, variable (not fixed, index, or single premium immediate) annuities do charge management fees. In fairness to variable annuities, if management fees are brought up as a negative, then full disclosure should follow, which is making it clear that mutual funds also charge management fees. Nobody any good at what they do is going to manage your money for free, be it through variable annuities or mutual funds.

If lowering management fees is an issue—then I want to go on record saying —m*anagement fees, whether inside an annuity or in a mutual fund, should be taken into account since it either increases or decreases the client's investment return. U*sing index funds should be considered. Index funds are not actively managed and are therefore generally less expensive than actively managed funds. I personally like to use index funds inside of variable annuities as well as mutual funds for my clients whenever possible. So for the record, when it comes to management fees, critics cannot pick on annuities without picking on mutual funds.

Next, let's look at Mortality Expenses (M&E) charges. This is the expense that gets the most press. I touched on this earlier and as I said, this cost can get expensive. M&E is charged by insurance companies on variable annuities *only.* This cost is to pay for the death benefit. I shared with you how the death benefit works in the Variable Annuity section of this chapter. The insurance company has risk, so they charge for that risk. Some companies charge more than others.

The truth is, the death benefit is a peace of mind feature for many retirees. It's a "what if" insurance policy. As I discussed in Chapter 1, while holding stocks for 15 years or longer is optimum, some in retirement are concerned that death will occur before a long holding period and heirs may lose out because of it. To them, the death benefit is worth the M&E charges. They are willing to give up return for the death benefit safety net.

While some want the death benefit and are willing to pay for it, for those that do not want it, they *do not* have to pay for it. Investing in a variable annuity does not mean that you are stuck with paying an M&E charge. If one wants the tax benefits that an annuity can provide but does not want to pay for the death benefit—no problem—it can be done. Similar to a 401(k) or an IRA, you can choose from an assortment of tax favored sub accounts (mutual fund type investments) to invest in at the same cost as a mutual fund outside of a variable annuity. In addition, like an IRA, the heirs can have the benefit of a non-qualified stretch at the owner's death. And there is no surrender penalty on the annuity.

Before you put your money into an annuity, do so as an informed consumer and you should be happy with the benefits you will receive. There is no reason to pay for something you don't need.

Another fee is an administrative fee. This is usually only $30 a year, depending on the company, and many companies waive this expense if a person puts more than $50,000 in the contract. The administrative fee is charged to pay for bookkeeping services.

Objection #4... *They have surrender charges and therefore you are locking up your money.* If you are on a diet, would it help if the refrigerator was locked during the times that you shouldn't be eating? Would you have a greater chance of becoming and staying healthy? When it comes to our financial health, surrender charges (if looked at correctly) are a good thing...not a bad thing. Studies show that when it comes to the boomer generation, saving has not been as high on the priority list as it was for the previous generation. A slap in the wallet if we take money out early, such as with pensions or IRAs, helps us become healthier financially, because it incents us to save. Our elected officials realize that we need all the help we can get to save for the long-term.

Surrender charges work in the same way. Also, as I talked about in Chapter 1, buying and holding stocks for the long-term is the smart way to go. A surrender charge adds another layer of incentive to ride out the highs and lows of the market helping to keep us from becoming our own worst enemy. I believe that surrender charges help us to become long-term investors as the facts tell us we should be. But again to be fair when comparing mutual funds to variable annuities, a B share mutual fund also carries with it surrender charges.

> *I believe that surrender charges help us to become long-term investors as the facts tell us we should be.*

For those concerned about surrender charges, there are some simple answers: *First,* have a cash-flow analysis done and determine when you will need the money. Then leave it alone until you need it. Make sure the surrender charge period is over when you do need it. You might be saying, "Yeah, but what if I need income before the surrender charge period is over?" There are ways to mitigate or eliminate charges if you know how to go about it.

IF YOU ARE STILL A SKEPTIC

In his book *Getting Started in Annuities,* Gordon Williamson refers to a study conducted by Morningstar in 1992. Morningstar is a leading provider of independent investment research in the United States and in major international markets, and is a widely used resource for the investment community. In the study, Morningstar compared the performance of mutual funds and variable annuities when taking into account their respective operating expenses which included the variable annuities M&E charges. The study assumed the investors were in the same tax bracket and received the same return. It further assumed neither had any surrender charges and that when the money was distributed from the annuity it was annuitized. It took only two years for the variable annuity to start outpacing the mutual fund. When the study compared other categories between mutual funds and variable annuities, in all scenarios the variable annuity beat out mutual funds after 2 to 5 years. When investing for the long-term, variable annuities are hard to beat. Rita was surprised to find out that by using *the right* annuity:

1. She and Stan could receive the same tax deferred benefit they received from their retirement accounts.

2. At the time they needed income—unlike the retirement funds where 100% is taxed at ordinary income tax rates—they would not have to pay ordinary income tax on the majority of the money.

3. They would not have to pay the high fees that concerned them.

4. If they passed away prior to using all of the money in the annuity, the children could use a stretch option, just like an IRA.

Rita gained a whole new appreciation for annuities. For the money the plan showed Stan and Rita would probably need for income, the annuity made the most sense. For the money that would probably be passed on to the children, a tax managed bucket was the best fit, allowing the children to receive a step-up in basis.

Some food for thought regarding negative comments about annuities; if annuities are so bad and so expensive, why do organizations like TIAA-CREF use them as the funding vehicles for their employee qualified retirement plans? I don't think such a big organization would shoot themselves in the foot by providing poor investment choices for teachers. And even though AARP makes money from marketing annuities, I think you would probably agree that promoting negative investment options may sully their reputation as being a light-house for retirees. Annuities, if used and sold correctly, have a place in the retirement market.

I hope this section helped you see that you do not need to be a victim of the negatives seen in print. Be an informed consumer.

IMPORTANT ADVICE FOR POTENTIAL OR CURRENT ANNUITY OWNERS

JAN AND ROGER'S STORY

Jan and Roger came to me because they wanted to find out if they had made the right choice by purchasing an annuity. Roger especially did not want to pay any more in taxes then he had to, so he thought an annuity was a good choice. He said "I have paid taxes all of my life and now that I am retired, somebody else can pay the tab. Jan and I have done our share." Roger is not alone. Most retirees I have met with over the years feel the same way. I asked Jan and Roger, "What is the purpose of the money in the annuity." Jan's response was, "We don't need the money now, but if we have health problems in the future, we want to make sure that it is available." I asked, as I do with all annuity reviews "If one of you passed away, who do you want the money to go to?" They both said, "Each other of course."

I did some checking with the insurance company that issued the policy. What I found out was, if Roger were to pass away before Jan, the money would bypass Jan and go directly to their children.

> *What I found out was, if Roger were to pass away before Jan, the money would bypass Jan and go straight to their children.*

When I shared the information with them, they were surprised, and more than a little irritated. A critical issue was missed—*the paperwork was done incorrectly*. The application sent to the insurance company had some of the names in the wrong places. From my experience, this is not uncommon.

What Roger and Jan almost fell victim to is called "trigger events." Trigger events come into play at the death of the owner, annuitant, or both. When one of the key players on the annuity dies, a payout of the contract occurs. If the policy is set up correctly, the surviving spouse can usually continue the contract without having to pay taxes—if set up incorrectly, a surviving spouse may have to go to her children asking for her money back. Hopefully, if that happens, the spouse has a good relationship with her children and her children's spouses. Adding insult to injury, income tax on the deferred gain would have to be paid by the children—double ouch! In Jan's case, as with others, she would have had to appeal to her children to get the money back and would have gotten back less because of taxes.

From my experience, many annuity owners are not aware of what triggers a payout of the money in the annuity. Interestingly, some insurance companies have diverging policies regarding how they treat the payout at a death. Some pay when the owner dies, and some when the annuitant dies. In the case of Roger and Jan, the trigger event was a ticking time bomb. What went wrong? Both Roger and Jan were joint owners on the contract…so far so good. You would think that if one joint owner died the other could continue the contract, but not with this company. This company is not unique in how it handles trigger events. In this case, the payout would have been triggered by the death of the annuitant. Since Roger was the annuitant on the contract, if he were to predecease Jan, the payout would have gone to the beneficiaries instead of Jan. Roger and Jan had put their children on as primary (first) beneficiary thinking that only after they both passed away the money would go to the children. Apparently, the agent who filled out the paperwork was not aware of how the company treated trigger events. What we did to solve this problem was fill out a change of beneficiary form, and put Jan down as the primary beneficiary and the children as contingent (second in line) beneficiary. Roger and Jan were happy that they had the contract reviewed.

On occasion, a couple will own separate annuities. The desire to own the policies individually is many times for personal reasons such as an inheritance or one spouse liked the concept of annuity while the other didn't. Or, the money that funded the annuity was tax qualified, and therefore by government regulation, there can only be one owner on the contract. Whatever the reason, owning separate contracts, while not necessarily wrong or bad, can add confusion about how to correctly fill out the paperwork. Set up incorrectly, the fallout can be a mess.

Trigger events on insurance policies are often overlooked. This is such an important area for those who want to stay in control of their money. With rare exception, unless estate taxes come into play or sometimes in case of a second marriage, most retirees want the surviving spouse to receive the money before the children. Some will have a rude awakening, when they find out too late, that they have been disinherited. I strongly urge anyone who owns an annuity, to make sure that it is set up correctly. You won't regret it.

> *Trigger events on insurance policies are often overlooked. This is such an important area for those who want to stay in control of their money.*

KNOW THE DIFFERENCE BETWEEN THE SURRENDER CHARGE DATE AND THE MATURITY DATE—AS IT APPLIES TO A DEFERRED ANNUITY

I find that some annuity owners are confused between what is meant by the surrender charge period and the maturity date on the contract. Understanding the difference is very important. I have heard annuity owners say, "My annuity is coming due, what annuity should I switch to?" Often times it is assumed that the annuity has to be renewed at the end of the surrender period. This is not the case. The end of the surrender period simply means that if you take your money out of the annuity the insurance company will not charge a penalty.

Additionally, in order to qualify as an annuity, insurance companies have to put a maturity date on the contract. The maturity date relates to the age in which the owner has to take the money out of the contract or has to turn it in to income. The maturity age is usually 100 years old. It is important to note that if you are healthy and reaching age 100 and do not want to take the money out of the annuity, you can simply write most companies and tell them you want to extend the contract.

Understanding the surrender and maturity date is important so you are not mis-lead into believing you have to move your money. It would be a shame in this interest rate environment to move from an older fixed annuity that has a minimum guaranteed interest rate of 4%, to another annuity with a lower minimum guarantee. This rate means that the issuing company can never pay less than that rate as long as you keep the contract.

There are occasions when moving an annuity can make sense, such as a higher payout, a greater rate of return, or ownership changes for asset protection purposes. Sometimes it makes sense to move to another annuity for the reasons I just stated, but unless you can improve upon your current annuity, do not move it simply because the surrender charge period is up or you are fast approaching the maturity date on the contract.

HOW TO GET TO YOUR MONEY WITHOUT GOING TO A NURSING HOME

Less than 20% of those who need long-term care go to a nursing home. Most people receive home health care or live in a residential setting such as an assisted living facility. The majority of annuities have what is called a nursing home waiver. What that means is, if your annuity is still in the surrender charge period and you need custodial care (which is what one usually needs when long-term care is necessary) if you reside in a nursing home the insurance company will send you your money without assessing a penalty.

A nursing home waiver is a good benefit to have, but *there is a better way*. A few companies have modified their annuities to include a waiver of surrender charge if you need help with two out of six activities of daily living (ADLs). ADLs include transferring, dressing, bathing, toileting, eating, continence. Severe cognitive impairment such as dementia and Alzheimer's are also covered under the waiver. If two out of the six ADLs cannot be performed by the annuity owner and or annuitant—or in case of cognitive impairment—the company will waive the surrender charge. What this means to the annuity holder is that going to a nursing home is no longer required in order to get to the money in the annuity during the surrender charge period. Most people I work with would rather stay home or go to an assisted living facility than go to a nursing home.

A word of caution: an income tax assessment should be made prior to cashing in the annuity, waiver or no waiver. In some cases it makes more sense if the taxable income is not received all in one tax year, but instead spread out over several years. I recommend that you check with a qualified professional before acting on the waiver.

For the consumer, the ADL waiver provides more flexibility and options. With rare exception, I personally do not recommend annuities to my clients that do not have this type of waiver.

> *What this means to the annuity holder is that going to a nursing home is no longer required in order to get to the money in the annuity during the surrender charge period.*

INSURANCE COMPANY RATINGS

Before putting your money into an annuity, make sure that you check out the company. When you need your money, you want the company to be in business. I prefer recommending companies that are rated by at least two separate rating companies, and have at least an A by A. M. Best, an AA by Fitch Ratings, an Aa3 by Moody's Investors Service, or at least an AA by Standard & Poor's (S&P). Ratings are an opinion, not a guarantee. I also look at how long they have been in business and if they have had, and still have, a solid history of paying claims. You can find the information on the insurance company that you're considering by either contacting the ratings companies by phone, searching on the Internet, or going to your local library.

Many of the insurance companies have their ratings on their Web sites and in their printed marketing materials. Your state's insurance department may be able to provide you with this information or direct you where to find it.

SUMMARY

An annuity is the *only* savings and investment vehicle that can do all of the following:

- Protect us from becoming impoverished due to the high cost of long-term care.
- Provide us with an income we cannot outlive.
- Help us shelter money from the tax man.

Whatever you think about insurance companies, the industry is uniquely positioned to help us guard against longevity risk. Innovative and *new-style* products now provide retirees with a cost effective way to save taxes not only while accumulating money, but also when income is needed. Many experts in the field of personal finance are convinced that a life annuity adds the greatest security to retirees. Choosing the right annuity takes planning and knowledge.

Remember:

- Be an informed tax payer—you will be in for a disappointment if you expect the IRS to knock on your door and tell you how you can keep from paying taxes. Don't give your hard earned money to the government unless you want to. Each dollar that you pay in taxes erodes your financial security.
- We can learn from sage advice—never pay taxes on money that you don't need for consumption. In other words, *eliminate excessive phantom income, which is income that you receive from savings and investments that you don't need to pay for your lifestyle expenses;* doing so may keep you from paying tax on your Social Security benefits. Annuities are great tools to help you accomplish this.
- Get advice on how to design a pension that neither you nor your spouse can out live.
- Don't let negative press scare you away.
- Don't put money in an annuity unless it meets a need or solves a problem, in other words, don't be sold something you don't need.

- Like any business, there are good and bad ones and insurance companies are no different. Check them out before putting money into one of their annuities, or any insurance products for that matter.

- Make sure the annuity paperwork is filled out correctly, otherwise you may disinherit yourself or your spouse.

Chapter 3

The New Income Strategy...Providing Worry-Free Income for a Long and Uncertain Retirement

The Third Step to a Worry-Free Retirement

It's Not The Gross But The Net That Matters

You may have noticed that the majority of financial magazines and television programs focus on how to accumulate money but pay little attention to how to distribute it once one reaches retirement age. This is a problem....it ignores the needs of those that are currently retired and those who will be in the future. If we are to be successful in the distribution phase, there are three critical questions we must answer:

1. Do I have enough money to last my lifetime, and the lifetime of my spouse?
2. Is my money positioned correctly?
3. In what order do I use my assets to produce income?

The fact is, the strategies used to accumulate money are different than those used to distribute it. Therefore, in the accumulation phase, it is not necessary to ask nor to answer the three questions that are critical to our success in the

> *If we use the same approach in the distribution phase of our lives as we did in the accumulation phase, we may be making a big mistake…one that may not be able to be fixed.*

distributions phase. If we use the same approach in the distribution phase of our lives as we did in the accumulation phase, we may be making a big mistake…one that may not be able to be fixed. Here is an example: you may be familiar with the term "dollar cost averaging." Dollar cost averaging is a systematic investment strategy whereby the accumulator can benefit from market volatility. By systematically investing, let's say monthly, he can actually end up buying more shares for less cost when the market is down. Dollar cost averaging is a smart way to accumulate money over time.

What if we use this same principle to withdrawal money during retirement? Here is the problem: *the year in which we start taking the withdrawals can significantly affect our results.* Whereby, the accumulator benefits from systematically investing in a down market, the person taking distribution in a down market may be so damaged by the timing of the withdrawal that he or she may not ever be able to recover. Years ago a colleague learned this lesson the hard way. He subscribed to the policy, put everything into stocks and use them to produce income. The reason, since the market has historically provided the greatest return; he thought it stood to reason that it should also pay the most income. His

> *Success was dependent on which year one started taking money from their portfolio.*

clients who retired in the year 2000, and who immediately started taking income from their stock portfolio, were not very happy with his theory. Their money was in the wrong place and was at risk of not lasting a lifetime.

This point is driven home by a study conducted in 1994 by a financial planner named Bill Bergen. Mr. Bergen put to the test a claim that Money magazine made, that retirees could spend 5.29% of their portfolios annually without fear of running out of money. Mr. Bergen found that the *success was dependent on which year one started taking money from their portfolio.* If a person retired in 1972, taking an inflation adjusted 5.29%, they would be out of money after 23 years. If, on the other hand, one retired in 1966, they would be out of money in 18 years.

In a study conducted by Ameriks, Ph.D, Veres, and Warshawsky, Ph.D; titled *Making Retirement Income Last a Lifetime*, the authors evaluated conservative to aggressive portfolios running some 10,000 possible scenarios based on historical returns in order to simulate possible future outcomes. The authors concluded that while the aggressive portfolios have a greater chance of success when it comes to living longer, nevertheless, due to variables such as the year in which one retires, success is not guaranteed.[14] So what this means to a retiree is; it becomes difficult to recommend distribution strategies from stock portfolios with any confidence, because no one can say for certain what type of returns one can expect in the year that distributions starts.

> *In other words, it is not as simple as just taking income from a conservative portfolio or an investment portfolio. The former can cripple purchasing power over time and deplete assets while the retiree is still living; while the latter may create such a loss that we might not ever recover.*

Also, as pointed out in Chapter 1, a number of studies conclude that a common practice used in the past, which was to use a conservative portfolio made up of mostly bank products and bonds, if used today, may create a greater risk of one running out of money over time. *In other words, it is not as simple as just taking income from a conservative portfolio or an investment portfolio.* The former can cripple purchasing power over time and deplete assets while the retiree is still living; while the latter may create such a loss that we might not ever recover.

Another common practice of the past has been to invest money in a portfolio made up of stocks and bonds, and live off the income while preserving the principal. While this approach may have been effective in the years gone by, when it comes to living longer, it can create more risk for retirees. Here are some of the reasons why:

1. In order to provide the income that is needed, usually a large percentage of the estate may have to be invested in interest and dividend producing assets. This leaves too small of a percentage invested in assets that are needed to help maintain purchasing power. As I pointed out in Chapter 1, this can leave a retiree vulnerable.

2. It is usually not very efficient to allow excess taxation to chip away at the portfolio.

3. Commingling money into one big portfolio is not very efficient when it comes to distribution. The practice makes it difficult to

determine if money is in the right places and which assets should be used first.

Research bears out that if a retiree wants to eliminate longevity risk, the options I am about to show can provide more security. From my experience, it also provides more peace of mind. *If we are to create tax efficient income that will last a lifetime, we must focus on dependability of income.* If we don't, we might find ourselves having to either reduce our lifestyle, move in with the kids (assuming they ever moved out), or go back to work. In order to meet our objective of achieving tax efficient dependable income, we have to take what we learned in Chapters 1 and 2 and apply those principles. So let's review:

1. The shorter the time horizon, the more conservative the investment bucket.
2. The longer the time horizon, the more aggressive the investment bucket.
3. The longer time horizon investment bucket should own some stock to help protect against loss of purchasing power.
4. We must apply the power of tax deferral to help us build a bigger pot of money for when we need it.
5. Take advantage of the exclusion ratio by way of annuitization to help us achieve dependable income while further reducing our taxes.
6. An annuity will allow us to design our own pension.

Before we go any further, your financial future can be greatly influenced by what I am about say. You may come in contact with financial advisors who help people in the distribution phase of their life. While there are very good distribution planners out there, be cautious if the discussion of long-term care planning does not come up. I ended up creating my own distribution analysis model because I couldn't find one that integrated long-term care into the cash-flow analysis to my standards.

Not integrating long-term care ignores the biggest threat to retirement security and is a ticking time bomb. Anyone who thinks that an unplanned annual bill which can exceed $100,000 will not throw the average retiree's financial plan into chaos is smoking something and I don't mean cigarettes. This is such a critical piece of the retirement puzzle, like Glenn Close in the movie Fatal Attraction, can get ugly if ignored. Okay, back to taking income. There are three phases in our financial lives:

Phase 1- Accumulation (building an estate)

Phase 2- Distribution (taking income)

Phase 3- Transfer (passing on a financial legacy)

> *Not integrating long-term care ignores the biggest threat to retirement security and is a ticking time bomb.*

I have found that there are two types of people when it comes to phase two and three; those who feel that transfer is not important to them, and those who feel, while they want financial security, they also want to provide a financial legacy for family. From my experience, most people fall in the second category. Because of the two types of people, planning must be flexible to accommodate both desires. Therefore, as it applies to taking income, in order to meet the needs of both, two options must be available. Here they are:

1. Create a pension (life annuity) that cannot be outlived as the plan foundation with buckets to help preserve purchasing power.

2. Buckets set up in five year increments with no life annuity.

Let me explain the two options. While Option One provides the most security for the client, it may *reduce* the amount of the estate that can be passed to the heirs. The reason is, if the client dies prematurely, the money that was used to create the pension (life annuity), would die with the client (if husband and wife at the second death). Depending on how much of the estate was used to purchase the pension (life annuity), would affect how much would be available to pass on after death. For those who want the pension and *also* want to leave an estate it can still be accomplished. Two things can be done, which are:

1. Purchase a life option with a period certain. How this works is, if a life option with a period certain was purchased and the owner/ annuitant died, the insurance company would have to make the payments for the designated period of time. So let's say that a life annuity with a ten year period certain was purchased and the owner/ annuitant died at the end of year five. That being the case, the insurance company would pay the beneficiary(s) for the remaining five years. If this strategy is used, because the life option with period certain is more expensive for the insurance company (or greater risk), the insurance company reduces the income paid to the owner/ annuitant.

2. If the client(s) are healthy enough to qualify and funds are available, life insurance can be purchased to replace the money used to fund the life annuity.

Again, since Option One is used more for people who are not so concerned about passing on a legacy, the period certain option is rarely chosen. I stated that Option One provides the most security. Why? *Done correctly, option one can completely eliminate longevity risk.*

For those who want security but also want to pass money to their heirs, Option Two can be a better choice. While Option Two does not provide as much security as Option One, it is a close second. The secret to Option Two is to be very conservative on the bucket return projections and to provide the client with a secure non-fluctuation source of income for the first

> *Done correctly, option one can completely eliminate longevity risk.*

ten to fifteen years. To get a better understanding of how these two options work, let's take a look at them.

I debated putting actual client cases here, but even after changing the names, I felt it was a breach of client confidentiality. I don't ever want to compromise my client's privacy and my commitment to confidentiality. Also, there are so many variables when it comes to individual cases, I decided to take more of a conceptual approach in an attempt to keep it simple and not get embroiled in technicalities. Even though this book is not a fascinating novel, it is still my desire to keep you awake. I hope the following will give you a clear understanding of the options.

Option One) Again, this option assumes a couple whose first concern is maximum security. Often this option is used for those with no children, the children are successful and do not need any financial help, or the client(s) is not concerned about leaving money to the generations to follow.

Step 1: Determine income needs inflated over life expectancy.
Step 2: Take into account all sources of income, Social Security, pensions etc.
Step 3: Take inventory of all assets, separating out the investment assets.
Step 4: Decide on acceptable rates of return for each bucket.
Step 5: Put the long-term care projections in the plan.
Step 6: Determine income shortfall between needs and income sources.
Step 7: Figure how much of the investment assets will be needed to purchase the life annuity.

After completing Step 7, the plan will break out the number of buckets needed.

Now lets' look at Option Two; this option does not use a life annuity—instead it separates money into buckets to be turned into income every five years. Done correctly, Option Two can provide a great deal of security because of the conservative approach while still helping to meet the client's desire to leave a legacy for the next generation. After completing Steps 1 through 6 as shown in Option One, the analysis will calculate the shortfall between the income desired and the income sources. The plan automatically makes up the shortfall, separating the investment assets into buckets to meet the income shortfall in their respective time frame. How much goes into each bucket depends on the bucket's growth rate and the income needed from that bucket. So, for example, bucket #3 grows for 10 years to meet a projected amount and then pays income for 5 years. Unlike the method of putting all of the investment assets together and then living off the interest, the bucket approach takes advantage of our tax code by growing money currently not needed for income tax deferred to make bigger buckets, and then paying out tax efficient income when needed. This allows the client to keep more tax-free income. Remember, *it's not the gross but the net that matters.*

So let's take a look at the buckets. I will give a narrative of their purpose and some of the particulars. But before we take a look at them, please keep in mind that funding them is part art and part science. There are several variables that need to be considered before deciding which assets go into which buckets. One important consideration is if the money to fund the buckets is qualified or non-qualified. Each bucket is separated into five year durations to provide flexibility and so not to lock in rates for too long of a term. The following buckets are for illustration purposes only and do not represent an actual plan:

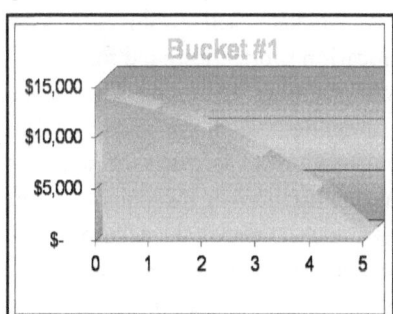

Bucket #1 is an income bucket. This bucket is to provide non-fluctuating, dependable, secure, tax efficient income, no matter the condition of the economy. In this example, the client put $15,000 into a tax efficient income producing investment, to meet current income needs. You can see the bucket is spent down over 5 years.

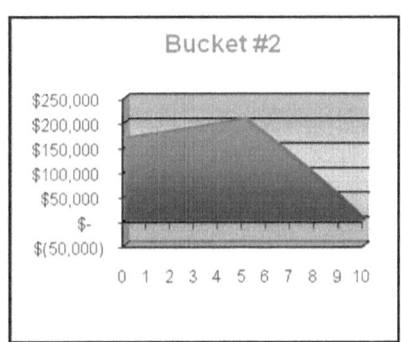

This bucket is designed to grow for 5 years and then be spent down. It is very important to fund this bucket with a tax efficient investment vehicle that will lock in a return, so there will be no surprises and therefore the client can depend on income without fail. Between bucket #1 and #2, the client can be assured of non-fluctuating, dependable, secure, tax efficient income for the first 10 years. These first two buckets allow the other buckets to grow uninterrupted, putting time on our side.

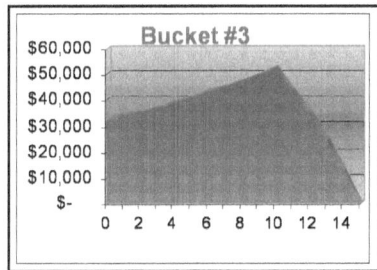

Bucket #3 is funded to grow 10 years and then be turned into income. With this bucket, the rate is usually not locked in because we have more time for growth since we won't need income from this bucket for 10 years. I usually suggest a product that will allow participation in the market upside without the risk of loss. I usually project a very conservative return for this bucket.

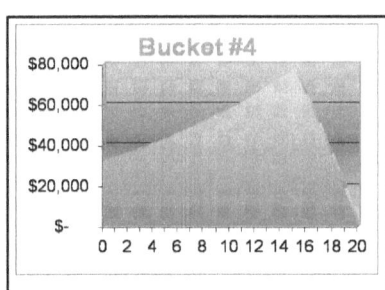

Depending on the risk tolerance of the client and the needed return, this bucket will hold an asset allocation model designed for growth over the next 15 years. The model is intended to help guard against longevity risk. Because of age and the 5 year bucket increments, there may be additional accumulation buckets to be consumed later in life by the client. That being the case, in addition to Bucket #4, there may be a Bucket #5 and #6, designed for growth.

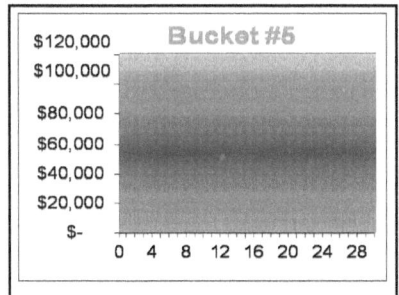

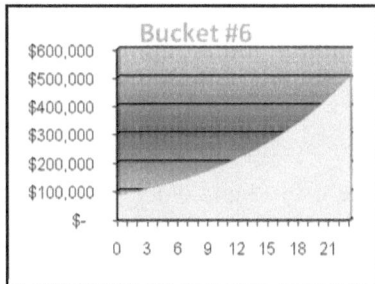

This bucket looks different than the other buckets because it holds assets to pay for long-term care. So when long-term care protection is needed and the client has sufficient assets, an alternative to traditional long-term care insurance can be more attractive for several reasons (see Chapter 4 for more explanation).

Bucket #6 represents money that probably will not be used during the client's lifetime. This bucket is usually funded with investment or insurance products that provide access if the client should need the money during their lifetime, but is designed to transfer tax efficiently to the next generation and/or charities at the client's passing.

A couple of important points when it comes to buckets:

1. The life expectancy of the client(s) will determine the number of buckets since they are split up into 5 year increments. When I say life expectancy, I do not necessarily mean life expectancy as defined by the IRS or an insurance company. I am referring to a number that the client is comfortable with. I have clients that want to project income out to age 100. I actually prefer to have my client's plan for a long life expectancy because it causes the decision making to be more conservative. It is usually better to have more money left over because of expecting to live longer than to run out of money because of assuming a shorter lifetime.

2. The returns used for each bucket should be conservative. One of the great things about the bucket approach to investing is it takes the guess work out of funding the buckets. Short-term buckets call for investments and products that are designed for the short-term, while the longer-term buckets are funded with more aggressive long-term investments with the returns reflective of the timeframe. Regarding the long-term buckets, I never estimate more than an 8% return even though historically the asset allocation models have

done better. Many people were bit badly in the 80s because of some in the financial community projecting high returns in order to sell investments. The public suffered because of that carelessness. Projecting high returns can build a false sense of security and can cause some to outlive their means, so it is important to be conservative.

The task is to build performance-optimized buckets to meet our retirement goals. The bucket approach to investing empowers us to apply the principles needed to help us defeat longevity risk. Those principles are:

1. Puts time on our side helping us to beat the crowd when it comes to investing.
2. Helps keep us from panicking when everyone else is.
3. Provides us with worry-free income that we and our spouse cannot outlive.
4. Allows us to use the government's money to build more security for ourselves.
5. Can help protect us from the cost of long-term care.
6. Helps protect us from taking income from stocks at the wrong time.

> *The task is to build performance-optimized buckets to meet our retirement goals.*

7. Answers the three critical questions:
   a. Do I have enough money to last my lifetime and the lifetime of my spouse?
   b. Is my money positioned correctly?
   c. In what order do I use my assets to produce income?

CRISIS INCOME PLANNING

It is critically important to address crisis income planning in any book that desires to empower people in retirement. What do I mean by "crisis income planning?" Often, a new client is referred to me whose husband or wife is entering a long-term care facility. The client wants to know if they will be able to private pay for care or if it is in their best interest to structure their assets so they can qualify for public assistance. While the steps are somewhat the same as in Option 1 and 2, there are some additional considerations that need to be taken into account when it comes to crisis income planning. One is the fact that when an impaired spouse is not covered by long-term care insurance, the additional expense can be devastating (see Chapter 4). It then becomes important to determine if the family is better off going on public assistance or private paying.

A planner must have the specialized knowledge and experience to know what factors may negatively impact either decision. This includes such things as how much of the assets are qualified (pensions, IRAs etc.) and who owns them. Also, which spouse receives what income and from what sources.

Another area that is often overlooked is how assets are owned. It is my common practice to move ownership over to the healthy spouse whether the impaired spouse is on public assistance or not. This is so important because, if the healthy spouse were to pre-decease the impaired spouse, the assets could be placed in a "special needs trust" for the benefit of the impaired spouse. In other words, the impaired spouse would have additional resources to provide him or her with quality of life without affecting public assistance. This is why it is so important to have your assets with companies that will allow a change of ownership from one spouse to the other without adverse tax consequences. I call this, being able to "flip the switch." Not all companies are equipped to provide this option.

As we live longer it is not only possible, but very likely, that one spouse will become incapacitated and therefore need care. *We must have a plan in place and our money positioned in such a way as to allow us to move quickly and efficiently if and when that day comes.* This is another reason that having a Power of Attorney and knowing how to own assets is becoming more important.

EVERYONE IS UNIQUE

> *We must have a plan in place and our money positioned in such a way as to allow us to move quickly and efficiently if and when that day comes.*

When it comes to income planning, as with any type of financial planning, there are no absolutes; each person's situation is different. As an example, I have a relatively young client who does not want any money in stocks. Because of her income sources, along with her income needs and the amount of her investment assets, after running my distribution model the numbers work out that she can meet her inflation adjusted income needs without having to own stocks. I have other clients, while normally very conservative—once they know that they have protected themselves against the risk of long-term care and that they have adequate income to meet a long life expectancy—they chose to be more aggressive with Bucket #6. They can do this with confidence knowing the money in Bucket #6 has been identified to benefit their children or grandchildren.

So, while the income principles provide us with a guideline and foundation for distribution planning, they still need to be customized to the client's wants, needs, and level of comfort. Again, planning is about peace of mind, which should be our end goal. Anything less can rob us of a worry-free retirement.

SUMMARY

- A life annuity can totally eliminate longevity risk.

- Option Two provides a great amount of security, but also accommodates those that want to leave a financial legacy for children, grandchildren, or charities.

- A single portfolio made up of stocks and bonds may not be adequate to help guard against longevity risk, and is usually not very efficient.

- It is dangerous to take money at the wrong time from a portfolio that contains stocks.

- It's not the gross but the net that matters.

- The ability to shift asset ownership is critical to help protect ourselves and our spouses from becoming impoverished. We need to be in the position to be able to "flip the switch".

- We must use a distribution analysis model that takes into account the possible cost of long-term care and is designed to answer the three critical questions:

  o Do I have enough money to last my lifetime and the lifetime of my spouse?

  o Is my money positioned correctly?

  o In what order do I use my assets to produce income?

- The task is to build performance-optimized buckets to meet our retirement goals.

Chapter 4

How to Protect Yourself from the Devastating Cost of Long-Term Care

The Fourth Step to a Worry-Free Retirement

"A stitch in time saves nine."
- Benjamin Franklin

"If I knew I was going to live this long I would have taken better care of myself."
- Mickey Mantle

Emily entered the nursing home in January of 2003 at the age of 89. Emily has a multitude of health problems including Parkinson's disease, poor eyesight, incontinence, depression, and is confined to a wheel chair. Her husband, who worked as a salesperson for a home builder, has been in a caregiver role for many years. After several attempts to provide around-the clock nursing care at home, Emily's husband decided he could no longer meet his wife's needs there—even with the support of full-time nurses. *"I had spent an awful lot of money [paying for care at home]. That was my biggest expense. Had it 'round the clock. Had to. I could not help her to the bathroom."* Emily entered the nursing home as a private paying resident and within 5 months spent down to Medicaid eligibility. Before qualifying for Medicaid, Emily and her husband had modest assets—in the form of CDs, stocks and IRAs—but 24/7 nursing care for several years at home, followed by the monthly $6,000 cost of nursing home care, quickly depleted their assets.[3]

An important reason I am writing this book is because of what happens to people like Emily and her husband. Going broke because of needing long-

> *Nobody should go broke because of needing care. It just doesn't have to happen!*

term care happens too often and it just doesn't have to. It upsets me! *Nobody should go broke because of needing care.* If you read *any* part of this book I hope it is *this* chapter. What you will learn, unfortunately, few people know. If they did, going broke wouldn't affect so many families. I have yet to meet with a family that wants to go broke. A study conducted by Marlene S. Stum, Associate Professor in the Family Social Science Department at the University of Minnesota, found in her study titled, *"Later Life Financial Security: Examining The Meaning Attributed To Goals When Coping With Long-term care,"* that families faced with long-term care *want to be self sufficient, financially secure, and in control.* The problem is, even though we desire to achieve these noble goals, the facts are, the majority of retirees haven't done anything to make them a reality. In her book, *The Complete Idiots Guide to Long-Term Care Planning*, Marilee Driscoll writes, "Longer lifespans make LTC almost inevitable." Shockingly, 78% of retirees enter the most financially vulnerable time in their lives without a plan of how to protect themselves from the number one threat to financial security in retirement.[15] Temple University professor Jack VanDerhei states in an article titled *Retiree Needs Outpace Savings,* "Having adequate long-term care insurance is the single most influential determinant of whether an individual will have a financially secure retirement." Nevertheless, fewer than 10% of the population owns a long-term care (LTC) policy .[4]

> *78% of retirees enter the most financially vulnerable time in their lives without a plan of how to protect themselves from the number one threat to financial security in retirement.*

My objective in telling you this is not for you to run out and buy a LTC policy, as a matter of fact, I want to discourage you from doing so unless you know you need one. I will share with you how to find out if you need a policy or not later in this chapter. Professor VanDerhei made the point of saying *adequate* insurance, which means that you may find you need a policy, or may find that you do not.

Our lack of planning and not knowing if we need insurance puts tremendous pressure on the government's entitlement programs. Public officials know well the effect that LTC will have on our entitlement programs if we as citizens do not take action to maintain our independence. This problem is so important, the government is trying to motivate the business community as well as individuals to purchase policies through tax incentives. Why? So we don't bankrupt the nation's entitlement programs, such as Medicaid. While I am a proponent of public assistance in order to help keep a spouse from becoming impoverished, we delude ourselves if we look to the government for our financial stability. If it is our desire to stay in control, remain self sufficient and to achieve independence, the financial planning community as well as citizens must have a better understanding of the following:

1. Does Medicare pay for long-term care?

2. Long-term care insurance.

3. What are creative options that you can use to pay for care if you do not have nor can you qualify for a long-term care policy?

4. The need to integrate long-term care planning into retirement planning

DOES MEDICARE PAY FOR LONG-TERM CARE?

Many Americans believe that Medicare pays for long-term care. Dr. Ken Dychtwald, in his book *Age Power*, refers to a study conducted by the University of Pennsylvania School of Social Work, where

> *Fifty three percent of the 1,000 surveyed responded that they believe Medicare pays for nursing home care. Dr. Dychtwald states that, "This misperception leads to confusion and frequently results in tragic outcomes."*

they surveyed 1,000 adults asking them a range of financial questions. *Fifty three percent of the 1,000 surveyed responded that they believe Medicare pays for nursing home care. Dr. Dychtwald states that, "This misperception leads to confusion and frequently results in tragic outcomes."*

Furthermore, there is a glaring misunderstanding of the difference between Medicare and Medicaid. Medicare covers medical needs if you are 65 or older, regardless of your financial condition. Medicaid is a program based on financial need that pays benefits *only to those who qualify*.

Boiled down to it's bare bones, Medicare pays for skilled care up to 100 days. Medicare pays 100% of care for the first 20 days. Days 21 through 100 require a co-pay; Medicare pays a portion and you pay a portion. In order for Medicare to pay, you have to receive your care from a Medicare-certified facility and a three-day hospital stay is required. In addition, Medicare pays only for skilled care, not custodial care. Custodial care activities are those needed to function on a day to day basis. Called "Activities of Daily Living (ADLs)," these include such things as eating, transferring, bathing, dressing, toileting, and continence. Medicare's limitations create two problems:

1) Many of our elders need custodial care due to aging and cognitive impairment such as Alzheimer's. These conditions don't require a three-day hospital stay, so Medicare doesn't help.

2) Activities of daily living don't require a skilled nurse, a doctor, or a trained Physical Therapist, so once again, Medicare isn't the answer.

Generally speaking, if it can't be cured or fixed outright, Medicare isn't going to pay for your health care requirements past 100 days. So now you know what the majority of the population does not know and that Medicare is *not* the solution for our long-term care needs. Although this topic will not make you the center of attention at parties, now knowing what you know will nevertheless help you better prepare for the future.

LONG-TERM CARE INSURANCE—WHAT YOU NEED TO KNOW

WHY LONG-TERM CARE INSURANCE IS IMPORTANT

Why buy long-term care insurance? I know of advisors who have said, "People don't need long-term care insurance because the government has a plan for us, and if we know how to qualify our worries are over." In my opinion, this advice is reckless! There are two good reasons why long-term care insurance is important:

1. No one knows what the state of government benefits will be in the future.

2. Long-term care insurance gives you more options

No one knows what the state of government benefits will be in the future. Long-term care costs ($91 billion in 2003) account for about one-third of all Medicaid spending nationally. Spending on nursing home care represents the single largest category of Medicaid spending, surpassing spending on in-patient hospital care and payments to managed care plans.

Continuing increases in health care costs, population aging, and growing demands for long-term care are expected to contribute to growing, and some believe, unsustainable public spending burdens.[1] Current debates focus on slowing the growth expenditures of entitlements *rather than how to improve long-term care protections for seniors*. Medicaid's long-term care services are a critical source of support for millions of citizens.

Slowing entitlement expenditures along with more restrictive medical and financial eligibility requirements *reduces* the chance that Medicaid will be available for those retirees who will need long-term care services in the future. In coming years, it is very likely that an individual or couple needing care will not be able to depend on public assistance (Medicaid) to foot the bill. Long-term care being the number one reason that elders become impoverished, the limitation of Medicaid has a direct impact on the well-being of retirees, especially those who are concerned about their spouse's financial security.

The facts are, entitlement programs are stretched and no one knows what benefits they will provide in the future. Later in this chapter I do discuss Medicaid planning as an option for those who need care and do not have long-term care policies. *The good news is for those that now need care and do not have a way to pay for it, Medicaid is currently a viable option. The bad news is no one can guarantee it for the future.*

Long- term care insurance gives you more options. Anyone who has dealt with paying for long-term care would probably agree that those who can pay for services with their own money, or with money from an LTC policy, have more options than people who are on Medicaid. From my experience, facilities open their doors wide for people with money to pay, while those on public assistance may be faced with being placed on a waiting list. Why is that? In most situations, the facility receives less money from the state than from private pay clients. Since most LTC facilities are owned by for profit companies, the bottom line is important if they are to stay in business. Naturally, the first priority for companies trying to make a profit is to fill their beds with private paying residents. Another advantage for those who have money is they can gain access to a facility by initially paying expenses either out of their own pocket or an insurance company's. Then after becoming a resident, they can go on Medicaid. Once on Medicaid, assuming they reside in a Medicaid licensed facility, by law the facility cannot kick them out. In addition, if the facility chooses down the road not to accept Medicaid patients (giving up their state license), management has to find another Medicaid facility that will take their Medicaid residents.

AN LTC POLICY DOES NOT GUARANTEE BETTER CARE

While those with LTC policies have more care options than people on Medicaid, *owning a policy does not guarantee they will receive better care.* Unfortunately, many people who sell LTC insurance try to make Medicaid planning the scariest strategy that anyone can use for those in need of long-term care. The story goes something like this: With Medicaid, your loved one will be shipped off to the ends of the earth, fed inedible leftover food, and put into a room that even a convicted killer would protest as a civil rights violation.

> *Owning an LTC policy does not guarantee that they will receive better care.*

Here are the facts: Medicaid licensed facilities cannot discriminate regarding the level of care provided to those clients who private pay and those clients who pay via Medicaid. Medicaid licensed facilities have to abide by the rules under Medicaid. Is it possible for a facility to play games and make life a little less comfortable for a Medicaid patient? If motivated to make the bed available for a private-pay client, a facility's staff certainly could do that, but they risk a potential lawsuit if their actions are discriminatory.

Even a bestselling author added to this misconception regarding the quality of care, stating in one of her books, "The spouse who needs long-term care is then sent to a Medicaid approved nursing home, which is not necessarily a place where you want to spend your last days." I take issue with this generalized statement. First of all, people on Medicaid can receive care without having to go to a nursing home. Second, some people due to health or affordability do not have, nor can they purchase long-term care insurance. I think it is an injustice to scare those who have no alternative but to live in a Medicaid licensed facility. My personal experience regarding the quality of care received by those on Medicaid (not what I read or what I heard from someone else) is quite different.

My father resided in a Medicaid licensed Alzheimer's facility. His care was excellent. The facility did a good job of hiring people who cared about our elders. My family had no complaints. Like my father, my father and mother in-law also have had a great living environment while on Medicaid. My in-laws, though on Medicaid, were moved by the good graces of the facility management to a larger apartment to better accommodate their needs. My father-in law passed away a few years ago and my mother in-law to this day resides in the same assisted living facility. My mother in-law loves it there and wouldn't think of going someplace else.

Over the years I have had several people referred to me that had modest savings and whose spouses needed care. In order to keep the healthy spouse financially independent, Medicaid was the best option. While I have clients who are very happy with the care their loved one has received in a Medicaid facility, I have other clients who are not happy with the care that their spouses received, even though they were paying out of their own pocket.

From my experience, the standard of care depends largely on the management of the facility, along with the involvement of the patient's family. Ultimately, it has a lot to do with the homework a family has done prior to placing a loved one in a facility, and how active the family is in the ongoing care of their loved one. I recommend visiting any facility whether it be a Medicaid licensed facility or a place that only takes private pay clients—do your homework— and then decide.

All that being said, here is the bottom line; *buying a long-term care policy does not guarantee better care for you or your family member; it does provide more options and easier access to some facilities.* So in my opinion, painting a scary

> *From my experience, the standard of care depends largely on the management of the facility along with the involvement of the patient's family.*

picture of Medicaid in order to sell long-term care insurance is self-serving for the agent/advisor. Long-term care insurance should be purchased based on need and the fact that we don't know what the state of Medicaid will be in the future, and that long-term care insurance gives us more options. But since not everyone can qualify due to health issues and some can't afford LTC insurance shame on us if we try to scare them or ignore their needs.

THE FIRST STEP BEFORE BUYING A POLICY

From my experience, too many people buy LTC policies and then discontinue making premium payments, which results in the policy lapsing. The reason being, they bought it without knowing how it integrated into their financial life. In other words, it seemed like a good idea at the time, but later they weren't really convinced they needed it. I can understand the motivation to let a policy lapse under those circumstances. To find out if you need insurance, a financial analysis should be completed. Some will find they need it, and some will find that they do not. The following questions should be addressed in your financial plan to determine if you need long-term care insurance, and if so, how much.

- What is the projected cost of care with inflation factored in?
- What is the risk exposure? Do you currently have enough income and assets to be financially independent if you should need long-term care?
- What assets (if any) would you like to protect for the next generation? Which assets are you willing to spend on care?
- What income will go toward paying for care, and what income will need to go to a spouse (if there is a spouse)?
- Can the policy premiums be paid for with current cash flow, or is a creative payment plan more appropriate?
- Will you be able to afford premiums if they increase in the future, or is it better to pay the premiums over a short time period?

After a thorough analysis of a client's financial situation and determination of goals and objectives, a qualified financial advisor can determine what's known as insurance efficiency. Insurance efficiency is reached by not having too much insurance, which nobody wants, nor having too little, which creates unwanted risk. From there, a qualified advisor can better determine what benefit amount is needed, what elimination period is best, what benefit period makes sense, the inflation factor to be used, and what special features (if any) are needed. I have found that a person is more likely to keep

> *After a thorough analysis of a client's financial situation and determination of goals and objectives, a qualified financial advisor can determine what's known as insurance efficiency.*

a policy that fits their personal needs, is affordable (in other words, paying for it doesn't change one's lifestyle) and understandable in terms of the role it plays to help provide financial security. So after the analysis, if the plan shows that you need it, then the next step is to choose the right policy for you.

IMPORTANT POLICY FEATURES THAT YOU SHOULD KNOW

Long-term care policy features can fill an entire book. Since my purpose is to address long-term care as it relates to "longevity risk" with a focus on how to pay for it, I will concentrate more on what I believe are critical issues of choosing a policy. While my approach to long-term care is holistic (how it integrates with all aspects of a person's financial life), for those of you who want a more in-depth look at long-term care policy features (which I would encourage), I have listed some excellent books in the "Notes" section. [13] That being said, here are some of the policy features that should be carefully chosen, based on individual necessity;

- *Daily Benefit.* The daily benefit refers to how much the policy will pay for long-term care services per day. I am floored by the number of people who have policies that pay the same daily benefit. This eats at me! Why? I think you would agree that it is *nearly, if not impossible, to find two families with the same income, assets (savings and investments), expenses, same health, who are the same age—then why in the world would they have the same daily benefit?*

  > *It is nearly, if not impossible, to find two families with the same income, assets (savings and investments), expenses, same health, who are the same age—-that being the case then why in the world would they have the same daily benefit.*

  My findings lead me to believe that the salesperson's focus was on selling whatever policy he or she could, even if it didn't meet the need of the client. I find no fault with the client since most assume the person selling the policy knows what they are doing. Obviously, the policy was sold to them rather than them buying a product which was needed to add security to their life. Once again, if the client doesn't know why they have it and how it fits into their financial life, many will stop paying premiums down the road, ultimately wasting their money. The point I am making is; do not choose a daily benefit until you have considered other important financial factors that are unique to you and your family.

- *Benefit period-* People often mistakenly think that the benefit period refers to how many years they are covered after buying the policy. This is a misunderstanding. The benefit period refers to the time between when the policy starts paying benefits and when it stops. For example, a person age 65 purchases a policy with a five year benefit period. Let's also say that she needs care at age 80. If she meets the policy requirements she will receive benefits for five years assuming she continues to live. So, in this case she received benefits from age 80 to age 85. When choosing a *benefit period* one should apply the same criteria used to choose the correct *daily benefit.*

• *Elimination period.* The elimination period, which can also be called the waiting period, refers to the number of days one has to pay out of pocket for care before the insurance company starts to shell out. The elimination period begins the day you qualify for benefits under the policy. A 90 day elimination period is common and one that I usually advise my client's to take. The reason is, most people can pay out of pocket for care through 90 days without causing a problem. Choosing a shorter elimination period such as 30, 45, or 60 days just increases the premiums. I would rather see my clients put the extra money in their pocket, then to give their money to the insurance company.

• *Inflation protection.* Health care costs are increasing annually at an alarming rate. What that means to those purchasing long-term care policies is, make sure what you are buying now will do what you think it will years down the road when you are most likely to need care. If you do not, you might be wasting money and better off not buying a policy at all. As an example, let's say Mrs. Thomas takes out a policy today for a $130 daily benefit. She doesn't have an inflation rider to counteract the increase in the cost of care in the future. By the time she actually needs care, the daily cost is $330 a day. If she doesn't have enough money from her assets, income, and policy to pay for care, she could end up on public assistance. Unfortunately, some agents have sold policies without taking into account the need for inflation coverage because adding on the cost of inflation, would potentially kill the sale.[12]

  When choosing an inflation option, you can select either *simple* or *compound.* Simple is cheaper because it grows slower and is therefore less expensive for the insurance company. It works like this: Let's say that your original daily benefit is $100 and the inflation rate is 5%. Each year you multiply $100 by 5% and add that amount to the original $100, so in this example after 10 years you have a daily benefit of $145. The compound interest option is more expensive because your benefit grows more over time than with the simple option. With the compound option, each year you multiply, in this case, 5% by the accumulated amount as opposed to the original $100, so after 10 years you have a daily benefit of $155.

To reduce the cost of a policy, instead of paying the extra for the inflation benefit, some people pay for a daily benefit that is much greater than they need today. The thought is that down the road when care is needed, one will have a larger benefit. While this option seems plausible, if a miscalculation is made and care isn't needed until later in life than projected, there may not be enough of a benefit to pay the bill. Most companies give you the option to increase your benefit amount in the future instead of taking out an inflation option today. This choice is usually very expensive and often times doesn't pencil out.

- *Home Health Care (HHC).* Not too many years ago, a long-term care policy was called a "nursing home" policy. If you didn't have enough money to stay at home, the policy would pay the cost, or some of the cost of a nursing home. I don't know about you, but the last place that I want to go is a nursing home. I have nothing against them, and I am grateful that they exist, but it is not a place I want to spend my days unless there are no other options.

    Fortunately, insurance companies have created policies that will now allow you to stay at home, called Home Health Care (HHC). Be careful if you decide to buy a HHC only policy. People do so because they can be less expensive and also because most people would like to stay home as long as possible. While at first blush that may sound reasonable, you may not be able to stay home for the rest of your days and may need to move to a graduated care community in an assisted living setting or eventually a nursing home setting. This is especially true for women since you usually outlive us guys. Often after being widowed, moving closer to family or shedding the burden of taking care of property becomes priority and therefore staying home is no longer desired. If you opt for a HHC only policy, you may not be covered if you eventually need to move to another setting.

- *The Choice of An Indemnity (per diem) or Reimbursement Policy-* Depending on the insurance company, you can choose between being paid back for expenses (reimbursement policy) or receive a specified dollar amount to be paid to you even if you have no out of pocket expense (indemnity policy). While the indemnity policy provides more independence, allowing you to spend the money however you would like, be careful to use the money wisely, or you may find that you have prematurely exhausted your benefit. Indemnity policies are fairly rare and can be more expensive because the insurance company has less control and may have to pay money to the policy holder over a shorter time period than with a reimbursement policy. The choice between these two options should be based on need and comfort.

CHECK OUT YOUR LONG-TERM CARE POLICY CARRIER

There are many insurance companies that sell LTC policies.[12] Here are some things you should know before choosing a carrier:

- How does their cost of insurance compare with other companies that sell a comparable policy? Be careful about choosing the company with the lowest premium. Low premiums can be a result of a company's willingness to underwrite people with questionable health in order to attract business. If you choose such a carrier, you may be paying a higher premium in the future if the insurance company hasn't fairly priced their risk exposure.

> *The financial strength and LTC experience of the company is very important.*

- You may pay premiums for several years prior to applying for benefits from an insurance company. Therefore the financial strength of the company is very important. When you need your money, you want the company to be in business and able to pay your claims. What is the financial strength of the companies you're considering? I prefer recommending companies that are rated by at least two separate rating companies, and have at least an A by A. M. Best, an AA by Fitch Ratings, an Aa3 by Moody's Investors Service, or at least an AA by Standard & Poor's (S & P). Ratings are an opinion not a guarantee. You can find the ratings for the insurance company that you're considering by either contacting the ratings companies by phone, searching on the Internet, or going to your local library. Many of the insurance companies have their ratings on their Web sites and in their printed marketing materials. Your state's insurance department may be able to provide you with this information or direct you where to find it.

- Experience varies between companies. Some carriers have exited the long-term care market for various reasons. Choose a company that has been in the long-term care market for several years, and that has a track record you can check out.

- What is its claim-paying history? Is the company slow to pay claims? Does it have a track record of claim denial? You won't usually get this information from the insurance carrier. Check

> *From my experience, what triggers benefits is something often overlooked by policy owners. You don't want to assume that money will be there if you need it only to find out later that the policy is more restrictive than you thought.*

with the Department of Insurance in your state to find out if the company you're considering has had complaints regarding these issues. This is another reason to consider companies that have strong ratings and have been selling long-term care policies for several years.

- In what condition does the insured have to be in before the insurance company will start paying benefits? Companies vary on what triggers benefits. *From my experience, what triggers benefits is something often overlooked by policy owners. You don't want to assume that money will be there if you need it only to find out later that the policy is more restrictive than you thought.*

SOME LONG-TERM CARE INSURANCE DON'TS

- *Don't buy an LTC policy because you believe it is a tax write-off.* The policy should be purchased to help protect your financial independence and stand on its own merit. Insurance agents and the media will talk about LTC policies being tax qualified and, therefore, tax deductible. Many policyholders are surprised to find they don't get a penny of their tax dollars returned by the government. Consider the case of Mr. Simms, a 75-year-old man in fairly good health who just bought an LTC policy costing him $2,500 a year. Mr. Simms has an annual adjusted gross income of $50,000. In addition to the $2,500 in LTC premiums, he has $500 in medical expenses, for an annual total of $3,000. Since only those medical expenses over 7.5% of his income are deductible, Mr. Simms was disappointed to learn that none of his premiums will be reimbursed by the government because only the amount over $3,750 would be deductible ($50,000 @ 7.5% = $3,750).

In some cases, not all of the premiums paid can be included as a medical expense for the purpose of calculating the available tax deduction. For example, in the year 2008, the IRS limits the amount of premiums that a person age 75 can claim for tax purposes up to

$3,850. So if Mr. Simm's insurance premiums were $4,000 a year, only $3,850 could be added to his medical expenses to determine his medical deduction. Also, the amount of premiums that can be deducted varies with age.

- *Don't buy a policy just because your friend has one-* you may pay for something that makes no sense for you to own resulting in wasting money that could be invested to help create more security.

- *Don't buy policy add-ons (bells and whistles) unless you know you need them-* you may end up adding a lot of cost, increasing your premiums for no good reason.

WHAT ARE OTHER CREATIVE OPTIONS TO PAY FOR CARE IF YOU DO NOT HAVE, NOR CAN YOU QUALIFY, FOR A LONG-TERM CARE POLICY?

Joan and William Cross (not their real names) lived an active life. During their working years they spent their vacations camping and fishing, a passion that continued into retirement. Prior to retirement, they owned their own business, one that provided an income that met their living expenses and allowed them to put away a modest amount of savings for retirement. As they tried to save, they raised three children and helped put them through college. With their house paid for and no debt, the monthly Social Security checks combined with their savings and modest inflation should have proven adequate to carry them through the rest of their lives. But like most Americans, they didn't foresee or plan for what would occur over time.

William and Joan started to notice that William was becoming more forgetful. One of their worst fears was confirmed when William was diagnosed with Alzheimer's. Sadly, he was becoming increasingly aware of what the future was to bring. He started selling the hunting and fishing gear that had been such an important part of his life. Unfortunately, Joan and William didn't plan for the additional cost for such a major health care issue—one that is knocking on more and more of our elder's doors. Their children, who had children of their own, were living in other states; Joan knew they had financial stress, too. Besides, the children weren't qualified to give their father the care he needed.

Joan continued to care for William until his condition required professional help. Like so many others, she needed answers to two critical questions: Will my husband receive quality care? Will we have enough money to sustain both of us? When she could no longer feed him or easily help him into bed or on and off the toilet, Joan discovered that she was faced with over $6000 a month in costs—that included the cost for William's care and Joan's monthly living expenses.

Like the Cross family, if you haven't done any planning to protect yourself from the high cost of long-term care, you should find this section invaluable. From my experience, many people believe that either you own a long-term care policy or you risk spending down all of your savings to the level of impoverishment. That isn't the case. *For those currently with loved ones without insurance in facilities or those who can't qualify for insurance due to health problems, don't be discouraged—you may still be able to remain financially independent.*

> *For those currently with loved ones without insurance in facilities or those who can't qualify for insurance due to health problems, don't be discouraged—you may still be able to remain financially independent.*

My motivation for writing this part of the chapter comes from the many people that I have helped by showing them how to protect their life savings. The number of classes and seminars I have conducted on this subject reinforces the fact that the vast majority of the public is misinformed about how to protect their financial independence when faced with long-term care issues. My education through the College of Financial Planning focused on risk management, investments, income tax planning, retirement, and estate planning, but the new retirement planning frontier also calls for a working knowledge and experience in how to incorporate what the college teaches as it applies to planning for long-term care and the options available.

As a Certified Financial Planner™, I have studied and worked with other professionals to apply asset protection strategies to keep my family financially independent and to help others do the same. Over the years I have had the privilege of advising many families on how to remain financially independent. I help people with modest to large net worth's, and I have found that all of my clients have a common theme: "I want to be and stay in control and maintain my financial independence in any given situation." My passion is to help them do just that! If you get just one thing from this book, I hope the one thing is; *you do not have to go broke in order to pay for long-term care no matter how much money you have.* Let me repeat, *you do not have to go broke in order to pay for long-term care no matter how much money you have.* Don't let anyone tell you any different.

President Lyndon B. Johnson stated in 1965 when he signed Medicare into law: "…Every citizen will be able, in his productive years when he is earning, to insure himself against the ravages of illness in his old age. No longer will illness crush and destroy the savings that they have so carefully put away over their lifetime so that they might enjoy dignity in their later years." No matter how well intended President Johnson may have been, the government didn't anticipate that Americans would be spending so much on health care due to rising costs and living longer.

The first step is to analyze your current financial situation thoroughly so that you can devise a plan for implementation. Depending on the results of the analysis, you may be able to employ various options. Let's examine some of the options available to a family *that cannot qualify for long-term care insurance* due to either ill health or limited finances.

MEDICAID

One potential option that's becoming more common as a means to pay for long-term care for seniors is Medicaid planning. I have experienced a myriad of misinformation surrounding Medicaid planning, so I'll provide you with clarification from my experiences over the years and the experiences of many of my colleagues.

Medicaid is a joint federal-state program created to help people with limited income and resources gain better access to health care. It operates within a federal framework but is implemented through state laws and administrative rules. There are nonfinancial eligibility requirements such as age, disability, and residency, as well as strict financial eligibility requirements. When one qualifies, the government will pay a portion of the long-term care costs for the qualified individual.

> *I recommend that you work with a competent financial advisor and elder law attorney who are familiar with the rules in your state before employing any Medicaid planning strategies.*

Be advised that the rules for Medicaid vary from state to state. Problems arise when the states have varying interpretations or are slow to comply with the federal rules. *I recommend that you work with a competent financial advisor and elder law attorney who are familiar with the rules in your state before employing any Medicaid planning strategies.*

Because this section is not a complete study on Medicaid planning, I'll focus on hitting the high points and practical applications that you can use. I will also point out some of the traps and misunderstandings. As much as I have tried to steer away from it, in order to describe Medicaid planning strategies used to protect assets, I must be somewhat technical in my explanations. If you think Medicaid planning may be applicable to your situation, the next step is to seek professional counsel.

HOW MEDICAID PLANNING WORKS

(The Cross case was in my book "Protecting Your Money and Your Way of Life." The numbers have been modified to reflect the up to date regulatory changes.)

Using the case of the Cross's will help us better understand how Medicaid planning can work to our advantage. How did we help Joan Cross remain financially independent? Let's start with their financial picture when I entered the case. William Cross received $800 and Joan Cross received $421 a month respectively from Social Security. Their total income was $1,221. They owned their home, which was valued at approximately $180,000. The Cross's also owned one car and had modest personal belongings. Their savings and investments, not including their residence, totaled $372,000, which was made up of a fairly conservative portfolio. Their monthly expenses, between the Alzheimer's facility for William plus Joan's living expenses, totaled $6,200 a month.

Projecting that William's care expenses would grow at 5.8 % a year (the projected inflation rate at that time) and Joan's expenses would grow at 3% per year with an after-tax return on their savings and investments of 5%, the Cross's would be spending down their savings which created additional worry for Joan (a 5% after tax return was used because that was in line with Joan's risk tolerance). To qualify for Medicaid, William must: be 65 or older, blind or physically or mentally disabled, meet income requirements, and meet asset requirements. Due to William's age of 78 and his advanced stage of Alzheimer's, he met the first requirement. The next step was to find out if they were eligible under the income and assets tests.

INCOME TEST

In the year the Cross's applied for Medicaid, the income that William was allowed to have in the state in which he applied was $1,809 a month. William's income was $800 from Social Security. Therefore, for the purposes of Medicaid eligibility, his total income was considered to be $800, which was below the $1,809 allowed in his state. So William did meet the income requirements. It is important to note that when applying the "income test," the spouse's income is considered separate. The rule used is sometimes called "the name on the check rule," which means only income that has the name of the Medicaid applicant on it is applied to the income test.

What if his income was over $1,809 a month? Would that in and of itself disqualify him for Medicaid services? No, because the state in which William applied is an "income cap state," meaning that an Income Cap Trust (also known as a "Miller Trust") could have been drafted by a qualified attorney, allowing income eligibility under the rules. Note: not all states are income cap states. Most states are "spend-down" states, meaning that if a person spends his or her income (less the personal needs allowance) on care costs, he or she would still be eligible to receive Medicaid benefits for the balance of the costs if the other requirements are met.

THE ASSET TEST

For the purpose of Medicaid qualification, your home, car, and personal belongings are exempt and not considered resource assets. In other words, in the state in which they currently reside, the Cross's are allowed to keep:

1. Their home (principal residence) regardless of value, because Joan Cross is continuing to live in the residence
2. A car (usually any value if used for travel to work or medical purposes, otherwise a limit can be imposed).
3. Personal effects, furnishings, and jewelry (some states limit the value of these items).
4. A burial plan *or* an irrevocable prepaid plan.
5. Funeral or burial merchandise such as a casket, urn, cemetery plot, or vault.
6. Medical equipment, such as a wheelchair, may be allowed in some states.
7. Term insurance of any amount and cash value life insurance policies, provided that the face amount is nominal.

Joan and William's home, car, and personal belongings are protected and are not subject to "spend-down." In other words, the Cross's are not required to spend or sell these resources in order to qualify for assistance. These are called "non-resource" or "exempt" assets. But they did have a problem. Under the rules, at the time of application, William could only have $2,000 of assets in his name, and Joan could have a maximum of $104,400, which is called the "Community Spouse Maximum Resource Allowance" (CSMRA for the year 2008). Since they had $ 372,000 of savings, they were $265,600 over the allowed amount. The $265,600 was considered a "resource or non-exempt" asset and therefore subject to "spend-down." If they had applied to the state under the current scenario, the state would have told them to "spend-down" the $265,600 and then reapply for Medicaid.

WHAT OPTIONS DO THE CROSS'S HAVE IN ORDER TO QUALIFY FOR MEDICAID?

1) They could shelter some or all of the $265,600 if the money goes toward an "exempt" asset such as a new home or auto. In addition, the money can be spent in order to make additions or repairs to their existing home. Also, if they had a mortgage on the property (which they did not), they could have used some or all of the $265,600 to pay off the mortgage.

2) Transfer the $265,600 to their children.

3) Transfer the $265,600 to a trust.

4) Purchase a commercial annuity from an insurance company.

5) A qualified attorney can sometimes convince the state that more assets are needed to produce income for the healthy spouse, so some of the $265,600 may be able to be protected through the use of a "spousal support petition".

Let's look at each option individually.

Option One. Putting money into an exempt asset such as a car or principal residence. Remember, when a spouse is living in the primary residence it is exempt and can be valued at *any* amount and still qualify under the rules. A caution here is that the healthy spouse may become asset-rich and cash-flow poor. It won't serve anyone's interests to live in a mansion with an empty refrigerator.

Would this strategy work for the Cross family? Yes, but the problem was that Joan needed income over and above what the state calls the Community Spouse Minimum Monthly Allowance Standard (CSMMAS), also referred to as the Minimum Monthly Maintenance Needs Allowance (MMMNA). So, even though she protected the money subject to "spend-down," she would have left herself with less income than she needed.

What could Joan have done to provide income and still use this strategy? After William's Medicaid qualification, she could apply for a reverse mortgage (to be discussed later in this chapter) that would have provided her with a lump sum of money or a monthly income. The problem with this strategy for the Cross's was that they wanted to pass the house to their children because of the sentimental value. A reverse mortgage doesn't preclude them from accomplishing that goal, because they could simply take out a life insurance policy on Joan for the value of the mortgage since she was still healthy. At her death, the lien could be paid off and the house could pass to the children. Note: If the life insurance strategy is used, the beneficiary on the policy should not be William. If Joan predeceased him, the money received from the policy would put William over the resource amount allowed and he would become ineligible to continue on Medicaid.

In the Cross case, the cost of life insurance and/or a reverse mortgage was not necessary because she could provide herself with the income and savings she needed by opting to use the Medicaid annuity. I will describe the option Joan decided on in just a moment.

> *The idea is to gift the money to the children in hopes that the money will be available when mom or dad needs long-term care. I believe this option, unfortunately, is often used without analyzing the potential financial pitfalls of the decision.*

The majority of the clients I work with, especially those who have lived through the Great Depression, tend to be savers not extravagant consumers. They feel more secure with having their house paid for and having some savings. This mindset makes the strategy of putting all of their assets subject to spend-down into their current home or buying a new one very unappealing.

Option Two. Transferring the $265,600 to their children. The idea is to gift the money to the children in hopes the money will be available when mom or dad needs long-term care. I believe this option, unfortunately, is often used without analyzing the potential financial pitfalls of the decision.

The government has made this strategy more difficult under the Deficit Reduction Act of 2005 (DRA 2005). Transfers made after February 1, 2006 are now subject to a sixty month look-back. Prior to DRA 2005 the look-back was thirty-six months. In addition to lengthening the look-back period, DRA 2005 changed when the look-back period begins. It used to be from the date of the gift and now it will not begin until:

(1) The transferor has moved to a Medicaid care facility.
(2) He or she has spent down to $2000 (in most states).
(3) Has applied for Medicaid coverage.
(4) Has been approved but for the transfer.

If Joan gives away the $265,600 to her children and then applies for assistance through Medicaid, she could be faced with a period of ineligibility. Even though the money is now in the hands of her children, the state sees it as if the money still belongs to Joan.

An important note: the period of ineligibility can be less than sixty months.

For example, if Joan lived in a state where the average cost of care is $5000 and she gave away $100,000 to her children for safe keeping, the ineligibility period would be twenty months ($100,000 ÷ $5000 = 20). A common misunderstanding is that this rule applies to transferring assets to a spouse. That is not the case. A spouse can transfer money into the healthy spouse's name without a period of ineligibility. We will take a closer look at this in some of the other strategies.

I believe the strategy of gifting money to children can work against a client's goal of staying in financial control. Sometimes when the parents need the money the funds aren't there. The Cross's have three children. Do they transfer money to the most responsible child or to all of the children in order to keep peace in the family? I am familiar with cases where a child (or children) spends some or most of the money intended for mom or dad's care for other purposes. Or, a child falls on financial hard times and uses their parent's money, intending to pay it back. Other problems might erupt if one of the children goes through a divorce; the gift, intended for mom and dad, could become part of the settlement assets, divided between the child and the child's ex-spouse.

Option Three. Transfer the money to a trust. A sixty-month look-back period of ineligibility is applied to trusts. The rules surrounding trusts are complex, but some basic points of clarification are important. This rule applies to "irrevocable trusts," not "revocable trusts" (sometimes referred to as "living trusts"). For our purposes here, I'll simplify the difference. An irrevocable trust, in principle, cannot be changed or revoked, while a revocable trust can be changed or revoked.

A revocable trust, sometimes called a revocable living trust or living trust, is not subject to the same rules as an irrevocable trust. The grantor still has complete control over the assets in a revocable trust. So even though there is not a transfer penalty for moving assets into a revocable trust, the assets in the trust may be subject to spend-down since the grantor has complete access to the assets in the trust. Some believe that since they put their money into a revocable or living trust, the money is protected if they should need long-term care, but this is *not* the case.

To further complicate matters, the government has carved out some exceptions to the trust rules. These exceptions are "special needs trusts" and the "Miller Trust" (also called the "Income Cap Trust") that we looked at earlier. A detailed discussion on the subject of special needs trusts is not within the scope of this chapter. Nevertheless these are important planning tools for those with disabilities and those in need of public assistance. A qualified financial advisor can help you determine how to best fund these trusts, but the drafting requires a qualified attorney such as an elder law attorney.

Option Four. Purchasing a commercial annuity. Many people are familiar with annuities. Some retirees receive a monthly pension in the form of an annuity. Others use annuities to help insulate their savings from taxes (see Chapter 2).

An annuity for the purpose of Medicaid planning is a more complex process with some potential pitfalls if it's used incorrectly. Let's return to the Cross case. To illus-

> *An annuity for the purpose of Medicaid planning is a more complex process with some potential pitfalls if it's used incorrectly.*

trate the use of a Medicaid annuity, you must keep in mind two important factors. First, when applying the asset test to determine Medicaid eligibility, a couple's assets are considered to be jointly owned. Even if Joan owned her assets in her name only and did not co-mingle them with her husband's assets, the state still counts them as belonging to *both* of them. If she gave any money away, doing so could detrimentally affect William's eligibility under the Medicaid rules. Second, because the couple's assets are considered jointly owned, a married couple can transfer ownership into the name of one spouse without affecting the eligibility of the other spouse.

The strategy is to purchase an annuity from an insurance company, but instead of purchasing the annuity for income tax deferral, one is purchasing it for income. In actuality, the $265,600 is exchanged for a stream of income. As the money is paid to Joan each month, she can take out what she needs to meet her expenses and then reinvest the balance to build back her asset base. An important factor is to make sure that the owner and the annuitant (the person with the rights to the annuity and the one who receives income) is the healthy spouse, not the spouse in need of care. If the annuity is set up incorrectly, some or all of the income may go to the spouse in care, which unravels the strategy and may cause the spouse in care to be disqualified for Medicaid assistance.

While the healthy spouse can only have a maximum amount of assets (which as of 2008, is limited to one-half of the couples assets up to $104,400), he or she can have *unlimited income*. In effect, the $265,600 is returned to the healthy spouse over a period of time through a series of payments. *A critical issue*: the annuity payments can be shorter than Joan's life expectancy, but they cannot be past her life expectancy. If the payout is past her life expectancy, then she will disqualify her husband from Medicaid qualification. The fact that the payout can be shorter than life expectancy, gives us an important planning option which is; the healthy spouse can recover assets relatively quickly by using a faster payout period. In fact, the annuity payment can be paid back monthly to Joan within a few years. When deciding on a payout period, the decision should have a rational purpose. I base the payout period largely on the income needs and the overall financial security of the healthy spouse.

From my experiences with seniors, it's not just about the money—the ethics and sense of fairness are paramount to them. We should all follow these principles when dealing with such important decisions as to who pays for the care of our loved ones. I feel a great sense of pride and purpose when I help those who have been prudent and diligent in saving money their entire lives, but find themselves faced with financial insecurity. In order to determine the payout period of the annuity, the following questions need to be answered:

1. How much does Joan need to pay her monthly bills?

2. What is the asset base that Joan needs to obtain and maintain in order to keep herself financially independent?

3. What is the savings and investment strategy that needs to be used to minimize risk while guarding against the loss of purchasing power over time?

I have found in most cases it is best to get the money back to the healthy spouse sooner rather than later. By doing so, he or she can reinvest the money quicker and build back their savings. Too many times, I have heard professionals speak of payments being set up over the life expectancy of the healthy spouse which, on many occasions, can be several years. Most times, that doesn't make a lot of sense. In our example, once William is Medicaid-qualified, Joan can use some of the money from the annuity payments to pay bills if needed, while the balance can be reinvested with the purpose of building her savings and security back up. The shorter the payout period, the higher the payment to the healthy spouse; therefore, more money can be reinvested quicker.

The only money that will go to pay William's care is his Social Security income. Joan can keep her Social Security income and use the annuity money for her and William's needs. Under DRA 2005, the states are allowed to be the remainder beneficiary on a Medicaid annuity up to the amount of Medicaid benefits received on behalf of the incapacitated spouse, which is even more reason to make the payout shorter rather than longer. If the payments are paid to the healthy spouse before the healthy spouse passes away, all of the money can be protected.

Why does a commercial annuity work under Medicaid? When Joan purchases the annuity, she is making an irrevocable exchange of $265,600 (her principal) for a stream of payments from the insurance company. Since she no longer has access to the principal, it is no longer considered a "resource asset" but instead it is considered income. Since she can receive unlimited income, her money no longer disqualifies her husband from receiving Medicaid assistance. Also, once William is Medicaid-approved, Joan can accumulate an unlimited amount of assets without causing her husband to become Medicaid ineligible.

Does *any* annuity purchased from an insurance company qualify as a Medicaid annuity? This is misunderstood by many who are not familiar with some of the technical features of annuities.

> *Some claim that by simply owning an annuity the money in the annuity will be protected from Medicaid spend-down. This is simply not true.*

Some claim that by simply owning an annuity the money in the annuity will be protected from Medicaid spend-down. This is simply not true.

In addition, some believe that an irrevocable exchange of principal, such as the $265,600, for an income stream (called annuitization) from an insurance company qualifies as a Medicaid annuity. Again, not true! Remember: if you have access to the money over and above the Community Spouse Maximum Resource Allowance, you have to spend it down before you can receive benefits from Medicaid. Just because you annuitize an annuity doesn't mean it qualifies as a Medicaid annuity. There are various qualifications that have to be met, but from my experience, the most misunderstood is *assignability*. In simple terms, if you can sell the annuity income to someone else on the open market and turn your income stream into cash, the annuity is considered a resource asset subject to spend-down.

I would imagine that most of us have seen commercials on television where companies offer to pay a lump sum to those currently receiving annuity payments. I, as the owner of the annuity currently receiving income from an annuitized annuity, can request that the insurance company *assign* my payments to someone else, such as the company on television. I sign an agreement and we work out how much cash the company will give me in exchange for the remaining payments. I, as the owner, simply request that the payments be sent to the company in their name instead of mine. Because the annuity is assignable, and therefore I can receive cash by selling it, the annuity is considered a resource asset subject to spend-down. That is why a Medicaid annuity must be *non-assignable*.

To qualify as a Medicaid annuity, the annuity contract should state: "This annuity is non-assignable, irrevocable, non-transferable, and has no cash value." An important note: A *deferred* annuity, is still considered a "resource asset" and is therefore subject to spend-down. Not until the annuity meets all requirements does it qualify for Medicaid. Unfortunately, many annuities are sold to seniors with the claim that they will protect them from the cost of long-term care. Be informed: *Unless it is a Medicaid annuity it can still be subject to spend-down.*

What's the downside of using a Medicaid annuity? In the case of the Cross's, they would have to liquidate their current investments totaling $265,600 and purchase a Medicaid annuity from an insurance company. If they had a higher percentage of their money in low-basis stocks or IRAs, for example, they may incur an income tax bill upon liquidation. An income tax analysis should be part of the plan before liquidating investments and purchasing an annuity. Obviously, the projected savings from the cost of care should be greater than the cost of purchasing the annuity. A full analysis should be done before undertaking a planning strategy so you can make an informed decision.

Option Five. Using a "Spousal Support Petition" to provide the healthy spouse with additional money. A court order to provide additional money for the healthy spouse also requires the employment of a competent elder law attorney. Some states are more liberal than others when it comes to such a court order. In some instances, the attorney can make a successful case for the healthy spouse to keep more money.

PROTECTING THE IMPAIRED SPOUSE'S QUALITY OF LIFE IF THE HEALTHY SPOUSE PREDECEASES THE IMPAIRED SPOUSE

What happens when the healthy spouse predeceases the impaired spouse? Although this strategy is out of the scope of this chapter, it should be part of the planning process with competent advisors. Sometimes it makes sense to have an elder law attorney create a "special needs trust" so that an impaired spouse will continue to have access to money—via a trustee—to provide him or her with quality of life. If structured correctly, such a trust can be a protective device that helps ensure money will still be there for the impaired spouse's needs; only after his or her death will the remaining money be available to heirs. If this strategy is used, make sure that the beneficiary and ownership designations are correct. Otherwise, the money may not end up in the special needs trust, which may cause Medicaid ineligibility for the impaired spouse.

THE USE OF A POOLED TRUST

A "Pooled Trust" can be used as a receptacle for assets of disabled individuals of all ages. The trust, which must be established by a nonprofit organization, must be a managed account for the sole benefit of the individual. Assets of the disabled individual can be placed in the trust and still allow the individual to receive public assistance, thus improving the quality of life of the individual. The assets in the trust can be used to pay for things that Medicaid doesn't pay for. Some of the ways the funds can be used are:

- Medical, dental, and diagnostic work not provided by public assistance.

- Supplemental nursing care, rehabilitation, and/or occupational therapy services.

- Expenditures for companionship and other expenditures that will improve the physical, emotional, psychological, and/or spiritual life of the disabled person.

The Pooled Trust is highly technical, and it's application is misunderstood by many. If the specific rules that need to be followed are violated, the beneficiary (disabled person) could become

> *In the case of Joan and William, doesn't it make more sense to keep one of them financially independent so that both of them don't end up on public assistance?*

disqualified for public assistance. In most cases, the assets remaining in the trust after the death of the beneficiary are distributed to charitable causes. How the assets are managed within the trust is determined by various factors, such as: the objective of the family regarding care for the disabled; legacy planning; risk tolerance; need for funds for the disabled; and the physical condition and life expectancy of the beneficiary. If the trust is to be used, a competent elder law attorney needs to provide the Pooled Trust Joinder Agreement that must be completed. Check with an Elder Law attorney to determine the rules for pooled trusts in your state.

STATE LIENS AND RECOVERY OF ASSETS UNDER MEDICAID

We covered "exempt" and "non-exempt" assets for the purpose of Medicaid planning. As discussed, the primary residence is considered an exempt asset with certain limitations under DRA 2005. States must attempt to recover costs against the estates of the deceased Medicaid recipients.

Many states have expanded their recovery efforts to include non-probated as well as probated assets. This can include the primary residence, but there are exceptions regarding the forced sale by the state of a primary residence while the Medicaid recipient is still living. In particular, most clients and family members seemed concerned about losing the primary residence or having to sell it to pay off the lien to the state. Many people want to be able to pass the family's home to the next generation as a part of their emotional and financial legacy. Through proper planning, this goal can usually be accomplished. Some states are more aggressive than others, so you should check with an elder law attorney in your state to become familiar with your state's policy.

THE CONTROVERSY OF MEDICAID PLANNING

Years ago, an owner of a long-term care facility said to me, "Dave, while I don't like you showing some of my residents how to get state and federal assistance, you are the person I would choose to help my mother." While not always popular, as an advisor, I use Medicaid planning for my clients when it's appropriate. The objective is not to put millionaires on Medicaid, but to use it as it was intended: to provide medical services for those in need. The term "those in need" is controversial to some, but I believe it's pretty straightforward when it comes to a married couple such as Joan and William. After an analysis of income, assets, expenses, cost of care, return on investments and savings, along with an inflation assumption, the numbers showed that Joan was at risk of not being able to sustain a lifestyle that would provide her with dignity and independence. An appropriate solution for Joan was to have Medicaid pay a portion of William's care.

Financial advisors are compensated for helping people make smart choices about their money. *In the case of Joan and William, doesn't it make more sense to keep one of them financially independent, so that both of them don't end up on public assistance?* Fortunately, Joan was still healthy; so we were able to use some of her savings to purchase long-term care insurance to protect her if she should ever need care. If Joan had spent all of her savings in order to sustain herself and pay William's long-term care bills, she wouldn't have had enough money to pay the premiums. Wasn't that in the public's best interest? I believe it was.

Under our current system, we have the right to use whatever legal means available to help ourselves and our seniors live a financially independent life. It's my job to lay out strategies and options available to my clients. As a financial planner, I advise my client, who is always the final decision-maker. Like some professionals, I have been challenged as to the legality of showing people how to qualify for Medicaid. I believe this is a legitimate challenge. You may be asking the same thing. Here is the answer. In 1996, Congress made it a crime to transfer money for the purpose of becoming Medicaid qualified. Labeled the "granny goes to jail" law, the outcry was so great Congress repealed it, but in doing so shifted the crime from granny to granny's advisor(s). In so many words the new law said, "Granny, we won't send you to jail, but we will send your advisor because he or she showed you how to become Medicaid qualified."

In 1998, then Attorney General Janet Reno, told Congress she would not enforce their new law because it was unconstitutional, violating the First Amendment protection of free speech. A US District Court judge echoed Ms. Reno's findings. As of now, the law remains on the books but is not being enforced. So, if your family or friends question Medicaid planning as an option, now you know the facts.

OTHER CREATIVE WAYS TO PRIVATE PAY FOR LONG-TERM CARE

One of the main reasons people looking for coverage decide not to purchase a LTC policy is affordability. For those who purchase insurance later in life, the premiums can be very expensive, especially if they are rated due to health issues. If you have to alter your lifestyle by tightening your budget to the point of discomfort in order to afford your premiums, you should investigate alternative funding options.

MANY TIMES, CLIENTS HAVE TAX-DEFERRED ANNUITIES THAT THEY AREN'T USING FOR INCOME.

After an analysis of their current cash-flow, sometimes it's discovered that a client would need to take income from their annuity only if they had a substantial increase in monthly expenses—such as the cost of long-term care. In those cases, one may be able to get more bang for their buck by annuitizing the annuity and using the income to pay the LTC premiums. The bottom line is, without adversely impacting their cash flow and lifestyle, they can use an asset to pay the premiums. Note: you will want to have an analysis completed before using this strategy because if you need income from the annuity later in life, although you can opt to discontinue premiums and use the income for other purposes, doing so would result in a loss of the LTC benefits. Why might an annuity be more efficient than another asset? For three important reasons:

- As I point out in Chapter 2, dying with a tax-deferred annuity often means that more income taxes must be paid. Why? Because children are usually the beneficiaries. The tax-deferred build-up in the annuity will have to be paid by someone. At the death of the annuity owner, the tax deferral is generally passed on to the children, who frequently are adults still in their working years and often in a higher tax bracket. The result is more money ends up going to the tax man. Annuities, along with qualified plans and IRAs, are not tax efficient vehicles to pass to the next generation. As I mentioned in Chapter 2, the good news is there are now some creative companies that will allow the beneficiary to spread the taxes over their life expectancy just like an IRA.

- Because the income from the annuity is paid out as part principal and part income, the tax can be spread over many years. This can be more income tax efficient than paying with other assets.

- If the annuity owner doesn't need care until past his or her actuarial life expectancy, the insurance company is supplementing the insurance premiums because they are contractually obligated to continue to make payments until the person dies if a life option is chosen.

AN ANNUITY THAT HELPS PAY FOR THE COST OF LONG-TERM CARE (LIVING CARE ANNUITY)

With the increasing fear that the cost of long-term care will drain the government coffers, annuities designed to help pay for the cost of care are expected to increase in popularity and availability. According to the Pension Protection Act of 2006 (PPA), in tax years beginning after December 31, 2009, distributions from annuities used to pay for the cost of long-term care will not be taxable when used to fund qualified long-term care expenses. Mutual of Omaha has put together a creative product called *The Living Care® Annuity*. It looks and acts like a regular tax deferred fixed annuity, but it has an important kicker; for every $1 put into the annuity, the individual (owner of the policy), receives $3 to pay for long-term care expenses. Mutual of Omaha's annuity gives several care options including home health care, homemaker services, personal care, respite care, adult day care, alternative care services, and traditional nursing home care to name a few. There is a catch; you have to be between age of 40 to 79 and you must pass some health qualifications. Also, there is a minimum premium of $50,000. After you are approved, there is a two year waiting period following a 90 day elimination period before the benefits start. The product pays a death benefit to your beneficiaries if all of the money is not spent on care, and like other annuities, it bypasses probate.

The Living Care® Annuity type annuity should be very popular with the retirement community for three main reasons:

1. Wisely, many people have money set aside that they only plan on using if they should someday need long-term care. This kind of annuity gives them greater financial leverage.

2. Most people realize that long-term care is a major threat to financial security, but they cannot bring themselves to buy a long-term care policy due to the cost.

3. They get the tax deferred feature of an annuity (see Chapter 2) with long-term care benefits.

IF PREMIUMS ON A TRADITIONAL LONG-TERM CARE POLICY ARE NOT AFFORDABLE FOR BOTH SPOUSES, YOU MAY NEED TO CONSIDER BUYING A POLICY ON JUST ONE SPOUSE

After an analysis of your assets and income, an advisor may determine that one spouse has more need of income if he or she should need care. This is usually the wife. With very few exceptions, women live longer than men. There are five times as many widows as widowers. Nearly one half of all widows are over age 65. In the Complete Guide to Health Services for Seniors, The Older Women's League estimates that in most instances, a woman's income will decline at her husband's passing, reducing the amount of money available if she should need care. [12] Due to affordability, it often makes sense to take out a policy on the wife and not on the husband, then position a couple's assets to protect their money if he should need care. By doing this, if he needs care, the couple can get help from public assistance. If she needs care, money will be available from her policy. Under either scenario, they may be able to maintain their financial independence.

FOR THOSE WITH LIMITED INCOME AND ASSETS, CONSIDER A COMBINATION PLAN THAT COMBINES PRIVATE INSURANCE AND PUBLIC ASSISTANCE PLANNING TO MAKE INSURANCE AFFORDABLE

> *With the increasing fear that the cost of long-term care will drain the government coffers, annuities designed to help pay for the cost of care are expected to increase in popularity and availability.*

This strategy calls for purchasing an LTC policy with a five year benefit. When the policy owner needs long-term care, the family could employ gifting strategies to protect the limited savings of the individual by having Medicaid pick up some of the cost if care is needed after the five years are up. The gifted money could be used to provide quality of life care for the individual. This strategy actually takes pressure off of the Medicaid system. "Among *Consumer Reports* readers, 43 percent reported in the 1997 survey that a relative in a nursing home had spent down and required financial support from Medicaid within the first six months they were in the facility."[12] Also, the facilities benefit financially because people can pay longer before having to go on Medicaid.

The drawback to this strategy is that no one knows what the Medicaid rules will be in the future. I believe that if our elders run out of money they would be entitled to public assistance, but I certainly can't predict the future.

YOUR STATE MAY ALLOW YOU TO BUY A PARTNERSHIP POLICY

After DRA 2005, more states have adopted partnership policies. While partnership policies can still cost the state money, it is a much better option than Medicaid paying the entire bill. Here is the partnership concept: to encourage the purchase of long-term care policies, *people who buy these policies can protect some of their assets that would otherwise need to be spent down in order to qualify for Medicaid.* Let's say that in your state, in order to qualify for public assistance (Medicaid), you can keep $2,000 in your name. So for example, if you purchase a partnership policy with a benefit amount of

$300,000, you would be able to keep $302,000 ($300,000 plus $2,000) and still qualify for Medicaid. This strategy can be effective for a couple of reasons:

> *After an analysis of your assets and income, an advisor may determine that one spouse has more need of income if he or she should need care. This is usually the wife.*

1. You can reduce the amount of coverage which in turn reduces your premiums.

2. The extra money can provide quality of life purchases while receiving Medicaid benefits. Here is what I mean; in most states, Medicaid does not pay for extras such as outings with family, extra food for your room, cable television, telephone, new bed sheets, etc. The extra $300,000 can help pay for some of your extra needs while still receiving public assistance.

3. Most people do not reside in a care facility longer than 2 ½ years. The longer someone can private pay the less cost the state will have to pick up, and for those who have policies that will take them past 2 ½ years, there is a good chance the state will not have to pay for any of the care. Note: Before buying a partnership policy check to find out the particulars for the state you live in.

AN ALTERNATIVE TO TRADITIONAL LONG-TERM CARE INSURANCE IS BUYING LIFE INSURANCE WITH A LONG-TERM CARE RIDER

This strategy has value to those who are not only concerned about the cost of premiums, but who also don't like the thought of their premium payments being wasted if LTC is never needed. Let's look at how it works:

- You pay a single premium into the policy.
- The money you put into the policy earns interest.
- If sometime down the road you want the money back, you can take it. If you take the premium back too soon, however, you may forfeit some interest, but you will never get back less than what you put into the policy.
- If you pass away and never need long-term care, your beneficiaries receive the death benefit, which is greater than what you put in the policy. They also receive it income tax free.

- If you need long-term care, the premium pays for benefits that pay out over four years, six years, or your lifetime.

> *People that buy these policies can protect some of their assets that would otherwise need to be spent-down in order to qualify for Medicaid.*

Consumer Reports states that if you have $160,000 to set aside, you may not have to buy a long-term care policy.[12] *What if you can get $160,000 of benefits without having to tie up $160,000 of savings? Here is how.* While this can work for anyone up to age 81 who can qualify, this example is for a 75-year-old woman who is in relatively good health and a non-smoker. She could put approximately $66,000 into a life insurance policy with an LTC rider which would pay her beneficiaries $80,000 income tax-free if she died, or it would pay out $160,000 in LTC benefits if she needed them. She'd still have $94,000 remaining to improve her quality of life or spend however she would like. The premium put into the policy always belongs to her, and she can access it at any time if she wants. Because this strategy doesn't affect cash flow and allows the lifestyle to be maintained, it can be a more efficient use of the client's money than self-insuring.

THE LEVERAGED INCOME STRATEGY

Elizabeth's (not her real name) family was concerned about her not having enough money to pay for care. Her condition deteriorated to the point where she needed to be placed into a facility. After she entered the facility, her expenses exceeded her income by $1,000 a month, or $12,000 a year. The family's main concerns were to make sure that mom had enough money to pay for care and that she could remain in the facility of the family's choice. The facility wasn't a Medicaid facility, and therefore didn't accept Medicaid as payment for care. As with some people who are in need of custodial care, Elizabeth's health was otherwise fairly stable. The unknown factor was how long her money would last while she continued to live. The family didn't want to take any unnecessary risks by putting together an aggressive portfolio in an attempt to make her money last longer. They wanted a predictable outcome.

If Elizabeth were to outlive her money, the family had a couple of choices. The first was to move her to a Medicaid certified facility. An important note worth repeating: My experience has been that selection can be limited when an individual is currently on Medicaid and is trying to gain entrance into a facility. The rules are different if a person is a private-pay client who goes on Medicaid in a facility versus being someone trying to enter a facility when she is already on Medicaid. The person already on Medicaid may be faced with a waiting list to get in.

The second choice was the family members would have to pay Elizabeth's bill. But her children had their hands full financially between paying their own bills and putting their children through college-- a fairly typical scenario.

In order to help keep Elizabeth financially independent, a strategy was used that leveraged her assets. This provided her with a guaranteed income of $1,000 a month, making up her shortfall. The income would be paid to her for as long as she lived. The strategy was to use an annuity that adjusts the payout based on health; the worse the health the higher the payment from the insurance company because of shorter life expectancy. The annuity was set up as a life option with a five-year period certain. Even though Elizabeth's chronological age was 82, due to her need for custodial care, the insurance company adjusted the payout to that of an older person—in this case, age 87.

This simply means that Elizabeth will receive income as long as she lives, but if she dies sooner than expected; the insurance company will continue to pay for at least five years from the date when the annuity was started. So if she died at the end of the first year, the beneficiaries would continue to receive payments for another four years. Elizabeth exchanged almost $79,000 for an income stream that she could not outlive. She was able to set aside the rest of her savings with the intent to leave some money to her loved ones or to use if her cost of care increased.

What if Elizabeth wanted more guaranteed income? She could set up a life-only option that would give her more income, but the payments would stop at her death. Also, some companies provide variable payouts that could potentially provide her with more income. Be forewarned though, the return can also go south. The "life only" option is used more often when there are no beneficiaries or the family is not concerned about money passing to them. The number one priority is to make sure mom and dad can pay their bills during their lifetime.

What if the family purchases a life option annuity with a period certain and down the road things change? Let's say that Elizabeth is still alive and they want to cash in the annuity. It used to be that if you annuitized an annuity, the action was irrevocable. Now there are a few companies that will allow you to reverse your decision. The insurance company uses a present-

> *As with any asset protection strategy, planning should take place before implementing a plan. You should always know the upside as well as the downside before making a decision.*

value formula discounted at a specified rate to determine what you will get back. It is important to know the formula before making the exchange, so you'll know up front what you're getting and what you're giving up.

Elizabeth's example has been simplified for the sake of illustration. For her family the strategy worked well because it provided a predictable outcome and they understood the risks involved. Before using any strategy, many factors should be taken into consideration. As with any asset protection strategy, planning should take place before implementing a plan. You should always know the upside as well as the downside before making a decision.

USING A REVERSE MORTGAGE TO PAY FOR CARE

For those people who are 62 and older and own a home, an option available to some people who need additional money to pay for care, is to tap the equity in their home by taking out a reverse mortgage. A reverse mortgage is the opposite of a conventional mortgage. With a conventional mortgage, the applicant takes out a loan and makes payments to a mortgage company in order to pay off their loan. With a reverse mortgage, the client uses the equity in their home to receive either payments, a lump sum of cash, a line of credit, or a combination of the three. Generally, the loan does not have to be paid back until the death of the homeowner or one moves away from the home (see # 3 below).

Reverse Mortgages have been gaining in popularity, especially with single females. According to FHA, HECM (Home Equity Conversion Mortgages) in 2007, 44.6% of the loans taken out were done so by single women. HECM loans make up about 95% of all reverse mortgage applications. These types of loans are insured by the Federal Government and the guidelines are mandated by HUD (Department of Housing and Urban Development).

Some states have tried to require home owners to first take out a reverse mortgage prior to applying for Medicaid. The problem with this rule is that in general, reverse mortgages require that the applicant reside in the home, otherwise the loan is due and payable. Obviously, many people who require care cannot remain at home. While a reverse mortgage may have some limitations as it applies to long-term care, it can be a smart strategy for those who can and want to stay home and need money to pay for their care or the care of a loved one.

A few key points to help you better understand reverse mortgages:

1. The age of the applicant (the youngest borrower), the value of the home, location, and the cost of the loan (including the interest rate) determine the amount of money that can be taken out of the home.

2. Even if one continues to live past life expectancy, she can continue to live in the home until she passes away. With a reverse mortgage, an individual trying to leverage some assets to pay for care has the security of knowing that one can continue to live in the home as long as she likes no matter how long one lives.

3. The mortgage has to be paid back upon death of the last surviving spouse, the sale of the home, or if the person permanently moves away. The homeowners have to continue to pay property tax, insurance, and repairs. If they fail to do so, the loan may become due and payable in full. Some states or counties have special programs to help with these expenses.

4. Bad credit does not prevent a person from being able to secure a reverse mortgage.

> *For those people who are 62 and older and own a home, an option available to some people who need additional money to pay for care, is to tap the equity in their home by taking out a reverse mortgage.*

5. The income from a reverse mortgage is not considered income and isn't subject to income taxes.

6. A reverse mortgage can affect eligibility for public assistance and can impact your estate plan. If a holder of a reverse mortgage lives long enough, there may not be any equity available to pass on to one's heirs. If leaving an estate is important, life insurance may be purchased on the healthy spouse if affordable. A "special needs trust" can be the beneficiary of the life insurance for the benefit of the impaired spouse if the healthy spouse should predecease him or her.

7. Your loan should be a non-recourse loan, meaning the lender cannot attach any of your family's assets or income, *except* the equity in your home.

REVERSE MORTGAGE AND HEALTH-ADJUSTED ANNUITY STRATEGY

If more leverage is desired, a combination of a reverse mortgage with an annuity (where the payment is adjusted based on health) as described in the section titled, "The Leveraged Income Strategy," can be effective. This approach will usually yield additional income.

USING A COMBINATION LIFE INSURANCE AND LONG-TERM CARE INSURANCE PLAN

As couples age, one spouse is often healthier than the other. Through proper planning, we can most often maintain financial independence. Using a combination of life insurance and long-term care insurance can be effective. Life insurance is placed on the life of the healthy spouse. The insurance also has a long-term care rider. If the healthy spouse predeceases the unhealthy spouse, the death benefit can be paid into a "special needs trust" for the benefit of the unhealthy spouse. Or, if the healthy spouse needs long-term care, the rider will kick in and make the payments. Special planning needs to take place to make sure there is ample benefit and income to cover costs if both spouses should need long-term care.

IF YOU HAVE A CHARITABLE CAUSE THAT IS IMPORTANT TO YOU, CONSIDER THE POSSIBILITY OF GIFTING LOW-YIELDING ASSETS SUCH AS HIGHLY APPRECIATED REAL ESTATE OR STOCKS

You can make a gift during your lifetime so that the charity benefits while you're living or designate a remainder gift to a charity, which is created while you are living but benefits the charity after your passing. This strategy might allow you to:

- Reduce your income taxes and have the government pay all or a portion of your long-term-care insurance premiums with the tax savings that you may receive.
- Avoid capital gains on the sale of the property.
- Increase income to help pay your premiums

- Eliminate or reduce estate taxes
- Diversify your assets to lower risk
- Increase your security while making a positive difference in your community

This can work well in conjunction with life insurance with an LTC rider. The assets that will go to the charity can be partially or fully replaced from the life insurance death benefit. Consider two important points with this strategy:

- If you need long-term care and use up the benefit in the policy, there may not be any money in the form of a death benefit to replace the assets going to charity.
- You or your spouse should own the policy as opposed to placing it into an Irrevocable Life Insurance Trust (ILIT). An ILIT will not allow you to access the LTC benefits in the policy.

INTEGRATING LONG-TERM CARE PLANNING INTO RETIREMENT PLANNING

Why is it that even though we want to be in control of our destiny and live a life of independence and dignity, the majority of us haven't done anything to make our goal a reality? Retirees enter the most financially vulnerable time in their lives without a plan of how to protect themselves from the number one threat to their financial security. When it comes to planning for the possibility of long-term care, why don't we heed the wise words that most of us grew up with, such as: "Never put off to tomorrow what you can do today." "A stitch in time saves nine." "Don't be penny wise and pound foolish." Rather than waiting until our family has a crisis, and then scrambling against the clock to remain financially independent, doesn't it make more sense to be proactive and plan for this threat?

To be fair, when I ask myself if I want to plan for the possibility that some day I might need long-term care, honestly I don't even like to think about it. But this does not concern just me…if I am to be a considerate, loving father and husband, I have to think about my family and what that day might put them through. If I haven't prepared, can I expect them to be prepared? Where will they be in their lives? What kind of problems might they be facing besides my need for care? Will they even be here on earth at that time?

I have heard from people over the years, "I took care of my kids and when and if that day happens, it becomes their turn to take care of me." But who in the world that loves their spouse and children wants, or expects for that matter, such a sacrifice from them? I know I don't. There is no doubt in my heart that in their love, compassion, and precious spirit, they would offer. As a loving parent and spouse, I want them to enjoy their lives... no matter my situation. Please don't think that I take this subject lightly. It happened to my father and it could well happen to me. I am not trying to impose my feelings on others, but I have seen over the years what havoc lack of planning creates.

So, I hope for the sake of our family's we can ask and answer the question, *where do I want to spend the rest of my life and can I afford it without expecting my loved ones to turn their lives upside down*? If we don't know the answer to this important question, then we need to find it out. Few people, including myself, want to think about it, let alone plan for such a difficult time in our lives. It takes courage to take this step, but if our goal is independence and dignity, we have to face down our fears and go forward anyway.

We may find, as many have, by looking at our options (which many times we didn't know we had), we actually become empowered to take charge of our futures instead of our future controlling us through fear. The place to start is through an analysis of your personal situation. A qualified financial planner can help you determine your smartest options. I challenge you to take the necessary steps to add more security to your life.

Note: an analysis is not only important for *pre-crisis* planning (prior to you or your spouse needing care) it is also important for *in-crisis* planning (if care is needed now or in the short-term future). Before considering *any long-term care strategy*, a plan focused on how to help you accomplish your goals should precede any action. Also, many times an effective plan can help you offset the cost of a long-term care policy by employing a properly crafted income and investment strategy.

A TOOL YOU WILL NEED WHEN IT COMES TO LONG-TERM CARE

If you do not currently have a power of attorney for your health and financial affairs, you may be compromising control over your decisions if you need care in the future or become incapacitated. With the help of a qualified advisor, you can either make these decisions while you are able, or run the risk of the courts deciding for you in the future. I would caution you not to go the do-it-yourself route, but to have a qualified attorney draft these documents on your behalf.

SUMMARY

- Don't think that Medicare pays for long-term care.

- Don't go out and buy just any long-term care policy. Have an analysis done to determine if you need insurance. If you need it, purchase a plan that meets your specific needs. If you follow my advice, you may save a lot of money over time.

- Do some homework on the insurance company and the person selling it to you. (see Chapter 6)

- Look for creative ways to pay for any insurance so you can have peace of mind. Knowing that if you need care you have it covered, and that you are paying for it

> *It takes courage to take this step, but if our goal is independence and dignity, we have to face down our fears and go forward anyway.*

creatively so your cash-flow and lifestyle is not negatively affected.

- Your health insurance does not pay for long-term care and as noted nor does Medicare. You have three options to pay for it:

1. Pay with private money
2. Long-term care insurance
3. Public assistance (Medicaid)

- Don't go broke and then go on Medicaid. Take inventory of your options before you are out of money.

- After an analysis, a competent financial advisor should be able to show you the numbers to either support paying for care with your own money or going on Medicaid. If Medicaid is needed, the advisor should introduce you to a qualified elder law attorney to facilitate the process.

- Giving away money or putting others on your accounts as joint owners to safeguard it may put you at greater risk of losing your money and not having it when you need it the most.

- Have your legal documents prepared now by an estate planning and/or elder law attorney while you are still in control. It is better that you decide your fate than the courts deciding it for you.

Chapter 5

How Predators are Plotting to Take Your Financial Security and What You Can Do About It

The Fifth Step to a Worry-Free Retirement

"The prudent see danger and take refuge, but the simple keep going and suffer for it." -Proverbs 27:12

"He who works his land will have abundant food, but the one who chases fantasies will have his fill of poverty." -Proverbs 28:19

While giving a financial fraud talk to seniors, I was tickled by the bold statement that one of the participants shouted. As I was carefully giving the audience some steps that they could take to protect against telemarketing scams, a sweet demure looking lady stood up and said at the top of her lungs "what's wrong with just hanging up on them, why waste our time being polite, just hang up." What good advice! Taking to heart the counsel of my friend in the audience would go a long way in protecting all of us from being victimized. In reality though, the problem with that advice is, most seniors were raised to be polite and trusting, making it very difficult for them to hang up on a caller. Not only do seniors find this difficult, that very sentiment also makes them a target for technology fraud. The tools of the trade for scam architects are no longer just the telephone, but they have also made their way into the internet.

When it comes to fraud, retirees are the target of choice because they have most of the money and they are usually home. The majority do not have answering machines nor do they screen by using "caller ID" and many feel it is impolite to screen calls in the first place. Therefore, perpetrators know the older population is more likely to answer the phone, and as you will see in this chapter—once that happens—the predators are very good at what they do.

Adding to the problem is the fact technology has proven to be a breeding ground for new fraud creativity. Many seniors have made their way to the internet and cons know they can be ripe for the picking. Contributing to cons targeting seniors, a study by AARP conducted for the United States Department of Justice, Titled "Off the Hook" found that fraud places victims in a state of tension and in order to resolve the tension victims may end up rationalizing their behavior by denying they were defrauded.[11]

This behavior plays into the hands of the con criminals exploiting the fact most seniors do not report crimes because they are too embarrassed to admit they were scammed. The best approach in fighting specific types of crime against seniors is being informed and taking the necessary steps to prevent these crimes from happening in the first place.

My intent in this chapter is to identify the typical psychological tools that cons use to get us to take the bait. Unfortunately there are a multitude of scams and trying to cover even the majority of them is beyond the scope of this book, besides cons change the content of their pitches along with what they are selling. Therefore, if I can help you better understand the psychological techniques employed by con criminals, you will be better prepared to thwart any attempts by perpetrators intended to take advantage of you. Also, I will include some of the most common scams and a few that were recently tried on my wife and me. The chapter will conclude by giving you some ways to help protect yourself. I encourage you to check resources such as AARP's Fraud Fighters www.aarp.org or 1-888-687-2277, your Attorney General's office, http://www.fraudbureau.com , or the Federal Trade Commission at http://www.ftc.gov . These are a few good places to start. Also, they can direct you to the correct locations if you have been or you suspect you are being victimized.

PSYCHOLOGICAL TRAPS

While attending a class on fraud, the presenters played an actual taped conversation between a senior woman and a con man. The conversation had been recorded by authorities after the niece had discovered her aunt was being victimized. A telephone relationship between the criminal and the lady had been going on for some time. The con man had discovered early on the woman believed that God expected her to help others. After uncovering this information, he quoted scripture to her in order to build trust and then started asking her to give money to what she thought was an important cause. What she didn't realize

> *When it comes to fraud, retirees are the target of choice because they have most of the money and they are usually home. The majority of seniors do not have answering machines nor do they screen by using "caller ID".*

early on was the cause she was giving to was him. When she told him she had no more money and couldn't give what he was asking, he turned on her and attacked her like a rabid dog brutalizing her emotionally and with no mercy. The tape was very hard to listen to; my heart went out to her and her family. How hard it must have been for her to be victimized not only by someone she thought was a friend, but to also be left broke and broken.

We may not like to admit it, but like the lady in the tape, we all have psychological or if you prefer, emotional vulnerabilities. We may feel compassion for the down trodden, animals, the elderly, or children. We may also want to believe in people and think the best when we hear what we think is good news such as "congratulations you just won." Our particular vulnerability is what the con man is trying to find out. He or she will direct questions at us in order to discover our "hot buttons" and once found, the perpetrator swoops in for the kill. He will look for our susceptibility to greed, fear, insecurities, or any exploitable vulnerability. If we are willing to listen to the pitch few cons miss their mark. The criminal looks for people that are naïve enough to believe they can get rich quick through a secret scheme or promises of a "no risk" investment.

Don't be mislead to believe only the weak and uneducated are victimized, there are cases where people our culture would deem highly educated discovered they too had just been taken to the cleaners. Dennis Marlock, a police veteran who has authored several books on fraud, tells us that from his experience he has discovered cons prefer intelligent people; they are more likely to have money and think they are too smart to get scammed.[11] A skilled perpetrator can be most effective when he comes across a person who prides himself on being an independent thinker believing he can never be duped. A prideful overconfident attitude can be our worst enemy. What is the message? Don't give them a chance to find your Achilles heel. As hard as it is for some of us, we should politely excuse our self and exit the conversation. Follow the advice of my friend in the audience, "Hang up the phone." If they call back you may have to get stern and if that doesn't stop it, report it.

Some years ago, I attended a class called "Citizens Against Crime". I learned a lot and the class was excellent. The instructor told us victimizers are looking for a certain type of victim. He gave an example of two people walking down a street; the first person we will call, Lady One. Lady One looks like she is very aware of her surroundings walking with confidence and authority while the second lady, (we will call Lady Two), is not paying attention to her surroundings, walking with shoulders slumped, giving a projection of weakness. Understandably, Lady Two is more likely to be targeted.

> *We may not like to admit it but we all have psychological or if you prefer, emotional vulnerabilities.*

The same applies to the phone, or an email. A take charge attitude will stack the deck in our favor. The con artist will more likely move on thinking you are not the weak person he or she is looking for. A word of warning, don't make the mistake of thinking just projecting the "need" to be in control is the same as being in control. If the con thinks you are a person that needs to be in charge, he or she will try to make you think you are when, in fact, you are not. Con artists spend a lot of time determining what type of individual may be most vulnerable to which type of scams. They learn by gathering information from victims and modifying their pitch accordingly to appeal to a specific type of person.[11] Therefore, once the con discovers a possible victim has a need to be in control, they will frame their pitch to appeal to that need. So when I speak of control, I am talking about actually taking it by halting the communication either by hanging up the phone or not opening an email from a source that you do not know or trust.[11]

To follow are some tools of deception that we should know about in order to protect ourselves from being taken advantage of—tools such as: reciprocity, herding, respect for authority, scarcity, likeability, and contrast.

RECIPROCITY

Many of us were taught to give back when we are given something. Most of us think this gesture is just being considerate of our neighbors. Cons know this and take advantage of this important value knowing that most people are fair minded. Here is how it works; you get a call that you have been selected to receive an opportunity to win a prize and all that you have to do is buy something from the solicitor. Although you do not have to buy a product under the bogus rules, the con is counting on you to feel the need to reciprocate for the opportunity to win a bunch of money. His company has done something for you *so you should do something nice for them.* If you fall for it, you end up paying for a worthless piece of merchandize or possibly worse, you just gave them access to personal information opening yourself up to identity theft.

> *Con artists spend a lot of time determining what type of person may be most vulnerable to which type of scams.*

HERDING OR FOLLOWING THE CROWD

I spoke about this in Chapter 1 as it applies to investing. Not only can "herding" hurt us when it comes to investing, but it can also make us vulnerable to fraud. Sometimes called "social proof", herding is common for all of us. In a fast paced world with much information thrown at us daily, we can gain comfort in what other people are doing. If we are "lead" to believe that our peers have taken the plunge and they have benefited, then it must be okay. Infomercials know the power of herding. It is not a mistake when selling a product, they will take calls from people who supposedly have bought and couldn't be happier with their choice. Infomercials are also famous for showing an ongoing count of all the people who have purchased the product reinforcing "social proof".

It is common for legitimate salespeople to use herding in order to build public confidence and trust in their products and services. The use of herding to get us to buy does not necessarily make the practice or the product they are selling—"bad." The product or service may be excellent and "authentic clients" are happy to endorse it. Many times when we discover a good find, we are excited to share it with others. Nevertheless, we should be aware of the practice and not be duped into assuming others have checked out the product or service for us, and we should always do our own homework.

THE RESPECT FOR AUTHORITY

While we need to follow the laws of the land and show respect for the proper authorities, we do need to be aware when it is being used against us for the purpose of bilking us out of money or stealing our identity. By triggering our respect for authority, cons can move us to do things that we normally would not do if not for a perceived power figure telling us to do it. Here are a few examples of the power that an authority figure can have over us.

In his book, The Psychology of Influence, Dr. Robert Cialdini, tells the true story of S. Brian Smith, a Viet Nam vet who in 1987 was protesting the shipment of weapons from the US to Nicaragua. Mr. Smith along with two other men notified authorities they were going to lay on the railroad tracks near the Naval Weapons Station just outside of Concord, California. The civilian railroad crew was given orders not to stop the train. The result was even though the crew could see the protestors on the tracks and had plenty of time to stop, *even so they did what they were told* and continued on. While two men escaped before the train ran over them, Mr. Smith was not quite so lucky. Both of his legs were severed below the knee. Amazingly, Mr. Smith did not find fault with the railroad crew saying that they were just following orders.

In AARP's, Your Fraud Fighters Handbook, they point to an experiment where a man standing by a parking meter dressed as a civilian asks people to put a dime in the meter. Not surprisingly, most people ignored him. He came back in a police uniform and this time the majority complied.

> *In a fast paced world with much information thrown at us daily, we can gain comfort in what other people are doing. If we are "lead" to believe that our peers have taken the plunge and they have benefited, then it must be okay.*

The two examples that I just gave demonstrate the power authority figures can possess. This power can be used by con criminals to get us to comply. Similar to a child following the direction of her parents, cons will often use authority as a way to persuade. In other words, we feel we need to comply with those that we see as "in charge". The exploiter may pretend to be a police officer or firefighter asking for us to donate to the fire or police department. It is natural for us to do so because we are being asked by someone we think has authority. The problem is the con is not helping the protectors of our society, but instead they are helping themselves.

We may be contacted by another con (or the same one) trying to sell us a sure fire can't lose investment. The perpetrator tells us the overseer of investments, the Securities and Exchange Commission, has approved it hoping we will think, if an arm of the government—perceived to be an authority—has validated it, the investment must be okay.

Awareness of this ploy should make our antenna go up when something doesn't seem "right". We can further help our self if we do not give money over the phone, but instead, ask for the caller to mail the information. Also, when confronted face to face, we have the right to ask the person to prove they are acting in an official capacity.

TIME IS RUNNING OUT! YOU BETTER GET IT WHILE YOU CAN—"THE SCARCITY APPROACH"

> *We do need to be aware when our respect for authority is used against us for the purpose of bilking us out of our money or stealing our identity.*

My wife and I have great memories of watching the movie The Lion King with our grandson, Xander. Some years back, I planned on buying it. In their advertisements, Disney said they would only sell it up to a certain date. I told my wife, "don't worry they are just trying to get everyone to go out and buy it now, it will be back on the market a few months after the deadline." I was sure that Disney was using the "scarcity" principle to motivate people to buy now, boy was I wrong. When we went to stores I would ask if it was in stock, but no such luck. I was shocked that Disney closed the door on buying the DVD not to reopen it again for some time (they may have now, but I gave up looking for it some years back).

In my business, there are times that the door is legitimately closing on some investment opportunities. Or we might have our eye on a house, knowing there is only one built in the location that we want. Anything scarce, be it a painting, baseball cards (I wish I still had mine from the 50s and 60s), a DVD (yes, Lion King), can compel us to grab it before it is gone, or at least we think it is. While some things that we know are scarce and to us have value, acting now to secure it, makes sense. Where we can run into a problem is when someone is using "scarcity" to get us to act now before checking out if what they are saying is true. As the pitch goes, "time is running out—you better get it while you can". Or, "there are only a few of these in the world, if you don't buy it now, you'll never have another chance." Infomercials use scarcity very effectively. They show the countdown with only so much time remaining to act.

A con artist will use scarcity to try and persuade you of the products value and try to motivate you to act before thinking it through. They try to make you believe someone else will snatch it up if you don't. The perpetrator will attempt to make you act now before you can get counsel, knowing that if you do seek counsel the con has just lost a target. I said target because the facts are, once you are taken, rest assured you will be targeted again by the same or some other con. You will have a bull's-eye on your back.

Buying something over the phone or on-line without checking out the source and the product can be hazardous to your financial health. Don't be pushed into acting. The more you are pushed the more you should be concerned. If someone physically shoves you, do you move toward them or away from them? Naturally, if they shove you with any force, you may not be able to do anything but move away from them. *Metaphorically speaking, the same principle should apply when someone tries to push you into buying something, the harder you are pushed the more you should move away from them.*

Scarcity has power in directing our actions. We may even desire something that we perceive as scarce only because we think it is. The same product, if thought to be available and that we can have if so desired, many times has no appeal and we wouldn't even consider buying it. Cons know that scarcity can move us to action even if under normal circumstances we may not even consider purchasing the product. Knowing this, scarcity is a popular tool for cons to use against us.

LIKEABILITY

We all probably agree that friendships are important. Finding people that we like and share things in common with can be a good thing. Once a friendship is established we tend to trust that person and think the best of them. While in a business relationship it is typical to work with those we like and who have similar interests—in the world of fraud—trying to create likeability is a tool many cons use to build trust with their victims. *The exploiter may agree with most everything the prospective victim says and he or she works hard to find or pretend to find mutual interests—we tend to like people who are similar.* The con may delve to find out about your hobbies, interests, passions, or information regarding your family—looking for things that he can use. His next step is to pretend he has the same interests, trying to develop common ground in order to help create a bond.

In addition to liking people when we have things in common, we can also be persuaded by flattery. Flattery can be a tool to appeal to our need to be appreciated. William James, a psychologist and philosopher

> *A con artist will use scarcity to try and persuade you of the products value and try to motivate you to act before thinking it through.*

said, "The deepest principle in human nature is the craving to be appreciated." Although false flattery is shallow, selfish, and insincere, we can still be affected by it. Studies show that even when people knew that the flattery they were receiving wasn't honest, they were still drawn to the person giving it.

If the con is successful and a perceived friendship is established, the perpetrator knows saying "no" to his request becomes more difficult. The person being targeted most often feels they may not be "a good friend" if they don't help out their new acquaintance by saying "yes" to his request. The perpetrator knows it is more probable that a person will buy from someone they resemble.

Liking others and having things in common, to many, makes life worth living. I have an instant connection with others that enjoy fly fishing, horses, Martial Arts, or with those who are in the financial world. I much rather work with people I like then those I don't. There are many credible business people who enjoy working with those who have common interests. As with many of the approaches that cons use, likeability is a good thing that can also be used for a self-serving purpose.

While there may not be a sure-fire way to know if someone is sincere, there are some things we can do and be aware of—such as:

- Ask questions to test their knowledge and experience in common areas of interest.

- Be aware if a bond is being created so you will buy something or submit to a request.

- Check the person's credentials so you know they are legitimate

CONTRAST

"Contrast" is a psychological tool used by many sales organizations. An example of contrast is a price mark down on an item for sale. The tag may show an original marked through price of $45.00 and below it in red shows the reduced cost of $19.95 plus another 30% off. Who can resist? Even if you didn't go to the store looking to buy that particular item—now you at least have to look! Car salesmen also use contrast in their pitch. Have you ever bought a car and ended up buying accessories such as an extended warranty, an undercoating, or perhaps a maintenance package for the life of the auto? Auto dealerships know if you take the plunge and buy a $30,000 car, purchasing these additional items in contrast to the price of the car, seems relatively inexpensive especially if it only adds an additional $20 a month to your payment. Or, take clothing stores, salespeople are taught to first sell the big item knowing if you just paid $500.00 for a suit, adding a shirt or tie for $40.00 in contrast to the price of the suit, doesn't seem like much money. Reversed, if you bought the shirt or tie first, buying the suit last would create a negative contrast.

Once again, the contrast principle is used legitimately in sales everyday which does not make it bad, but in the toolkit of a con it is another device to get you to take the bait. He might tell you what he is selling is being marked down by 70% and it has never been this low. Also, they only have x number to sell ("scarcity") and if you buy now you can lock in the 70% discount, but if you don't do it today you lose out never to get this opportunity again. If you say "yes", there is a good chance you will end up with a worthless piece of merchandise.

The power of these psychological weapons is the fact they can influence us without our even knowing it. We may not even realize principles like reciprocity, contrast, and the others, are being used because we have never thought about what they are and how they work.

SOME TYPICAL SCAMS

Scams come in different shapes and sizes. The more common approaches are charity, investments, sweepstakes, and foreign lottery scams. Some of the favorite techniques used in these scams are the following:

- *The element of surprise.* The plan is to catch you off guard so you do not have time to think or process what is being asked of you. The approach is usually a high pressure sales pitch telling you that you need to act now and if you don't you will lose the opportunity.

- *Gathering personal information.* The callers objective is to not only get you to buy what he or she is selling ,but to also gain access to your personal information such as you credit card(s), bank accounts, passwords, etc.

- *Requiring you to pay before you can receive a gift or merchandise.* You may be asked to pay a fee before you can receive the gift of merchandise. This may be in the form of a, processing fee, taxes, etc. If you get the gift at all, it may be just a piece of junk.

CHARITY SCAMS

This approach is especially popular when there has been a recent tragedy. The caller pretends to have been asked by some wealthy philanthropists to raise money for a cause such as the Oklahoma City bombing or the attacks on 9-11. Any calls for charitable purposes you should ask the following two questions:

1. What is the charities registration number?

2.   How much of the money goes to the charity?

> *The power of these psychological weapons is the fact they can influence us without our even knowing it.*

Tell them to send you the information in writing and you never make donations over the phone.

NO RISK INVESTMENTS

One of the most widespread problem areas right now in telemarketing fraud is investment scams. Many seniors are concerned about financial security making them more susceptible to investment fraud. The pitch focuses on an investment that is guaranteed to provide a substantial return with no risk. You may hear they want you to invest in the next company that will make you fabulously wealthy—all of your financial concerns will be behind you—and they have the inside tract to the next Microsoft, Wal-Mart, or Coca Cola. If you read Chapter 1, you know *there is no such thing as a return without risk*—the higher the return the higher the risk…period. If you receive a solicitation that focuses only on the return and promises no risk—and if you fall for it—you might as well kiss your money good-bye.

To help guard against investment scams, never agree to make an investment over the phone. Ask to have the information mailed to you and you will have your advisor review it. Tell him, if it meets your investment objective, you will get back to them. Always deal with people you know and trust and who have a track record that you can independently verify (see Chapter 6). Remember, if it sounds too good to be true it probably is.

SWEEPSTAKES

Who doesn't want to win a big prize? Cons know we are thrilled to hear, "Congratulations you are our big winner"! We have probably all seen commercials of sweepstake winners receiving a knock on the door and being handed a big check. It makes the process seem authentic—so when we see others on television winning the big prize, why not us? And as the pitch goes, if we buy products from the solicitor, the greater chance we have of winning a prize. So when we receive an envelope in the mail followed by a phone call both saying that we are winners—why wouldn't we believe it? *The bait is now set to get us to buy more merchandise with the hopes of winning more money.*

Sadly, one of my friend's mothers spent much of her meager savings purchasing magazines of all kinds in hope of winning the big prize. Many people wanting so bad to be big winners become hooked. They dream that by buying one more piece of merchandise, they too will get a knock on their door and handed a large check. The days of financial insecurity would finally be over.

To help protect ourselves from this scam, we need to realize that:

1. There is a greater chance that we will be struck by lightning then winning a sweepstakes.

2. Buying more merchandise is an empty promise which has nothing to do with winning; it only has to do with us spending our money on more and more product.

3. We are better served by investing our money wisely then falling for the sweepstakes scam.

> *To help guard against investment scams, never agree to make an investment over the phone. Ask to have the information mailed to you and that you will have your advisor review it and if it meets your investment objective, you will get back to them.*

FOREIGN LOTTERY

The Foreign Lottery approach asks us to respond to a letter which tells us that the overseas company that sent the letter has a secret way of selecting winning lottery numbers. If we want to find out more we just need to call a toll-free number. If we do, we are received by a very excited person on the other end of the phone. The person tells us this is our lucky day and that the company has reserved a number just for us. All we have to do to claim the winning number is to send them a processing fee. If we do so, you guessed it—no number and no response. They have just pocketed our money. As stated in AARPs' Your Fraud Fighters Handbook, "If a company or anyone had the ability to select the winning lottery number, why would they give it to you for a fraction of the winnings?"

Any of these pitches can be double indemnity for those that fall for them. If you do give them money, many times they have accessed your personal information. You may not only be out of the money that you sent, but also a victim of identity theft.

IDENTITY THEFT

More and more people are becoming victims of identity theft. The con is trying to find out your personal information such as your name, address, Social Security number, and credit card numbers. Here are some examples of how you can fall victim to identity theft and not even know it. A few of these have been tried on my wife and me.

I DON'T HAVE TO WORRY ABOUT CREDIT CARD SCAMS BECAUSE I DON'T USE THEM

I have heard people say they are not susceptible to credit card fraud because they do not use them. If you are or know one of those people… you will want to keep reading. Cons are hoping you believe you are immune because if you do, you will not be looking for this one. Let me start out by asking, how many credit card solicitations do you receive in the mail? If you are like most people who answer, it would be quite a few. Now here comes the scam. The con picks up one of your credit card solicitations from your mailbox—fills it out and sends it in. He waits patiently for the approval to end up in your mailbox and when it does, he takes the card and charges it up without you even knowing that he has it. You start getting the bill from the company who is asking for payment.

Skeptics may be saying" No way that can happen to me, only I have access to my mailbox. No one gets my mail without me knowing it." *You can still get targeted for this scam even if nobody can grab your mail without authorization and here is how—by way of your garbage.* If you throw away your mail, a perpetrator can grab the same solicitation out of your garbage can or recycle bin. You may be saying, "not me I shred my mail." While that is good—it might not be good enough. Some perpetrators are more than happy to spend several hours piecing your information back together. That is why, while shredding your personal information is critically important, the type of shredder you use is more important. Using a machine that shreds in strips is not adequate…you need to use a cross-shredder. A cross-shredder discourages a thief from trying to piece your personal documents back together.

So don't think because you do not use credit cards or you are the only one with access to your mail, that you

> *If a company or anyone had the ability to select the winning lottery number, why would they give it to you for a fraction of the winnings?*

are safe from identity theft such as the credit card scam. Remember, shred documents that contain your personal information and do so with a cross-shredder. Reduce the number of credit card accounts to just one if possible, so that you can track expenditures more easily. Every month, carefully review all credit card and banking statements; if something has been charged that you are unfamiliar with, notify the credit card company or bank.

FISHING (PHISHING) WHEN WE ARE THE PREY

If you have ever fished, you were probably more successful if you could fool the fish into biting by putting something on the end of your line that looked safe to eat such as a worm, piece of shrimp, a minnow, or anything to trigger the eating response. Similar to putting a piece of bait on a hook, Phishing, in internet terms, is where the perpetrator fishes (the "ph" is substituted for the "f" in fishing) with sophisticated "bait" in the hopes of "catching" important financial information. The phisherman is setting the hook to get personal information such as your password so he or she can gain access to your account. If you fall victim, while you may not end up on somebody's dinner plate, someone may well be feasting on the money in your accounts.

As our older population embraces modern technology, using the internet is becoming more common. A growing number of seniors are now shopping online and using email as a new found communication tool. While the internet has proven to be a convenient way to communicate, it also opens the door to the potential to be defrauded such as phishing. My wife and I know phishing well because it has been tried on us. Here is how it works. Masquerading as a trustworthy entity such as a bank, eBay, PayPal, or even the IRS, the perpetrator, sends an email to you stating they suspect someone may have tried to pull a fast one on you (aren't they nice and considerate) and they are putting a hold on payment until they hear from you. They ask you to click on their bogus website and enter your password. If you comply, you have just given them your password and therefore access to your account.

The Federal Trade Commission (FTC) (2004) defines phishing as "a high-tech scam that uses spam or pop-up messages to deceive you into disclosing your credit card numbers, bank account information, Social Security number, passwords, or other sensitive information. They may tell you they need to "update" or "validate" your information. If you receive an email from an organization claiming to be reputable, such as a bank, eBay or PayPal, give no response and simply delete the email. You will help protect yourself from this scam by always contacting the firm in question directly and never through a random request for information.

THE BOLD AND THE UGLY

Here is another one that was recently tried on my wife and me. We received an email from overseas telling us the author wanted to give his son who was traveling to the States— and what a coincidence, was going to be staying close to our home—some education about horses (my wife and I own a children's petting zoo and several full sized horses). He told us he would pay us a fee if we would work with his son for several hours over a period of time and he insisted he would not accept our help unless he paid us. We thought, "That is considerate, he is concerned about taking advantage of us (boy were we wrong) and wants to compensate us for our time and help." We said, okay, and responded with an offer. My wife said to me "What a good father, he is wanting his son to learn about the training and care of animals."

He struck a chord with me also, because I feel that working with horses can teach us patience, communication, and can be very therapeutic. We finally get a return email accepting our offer. He told us he would send a Cashier's Check and that we were to *wait until it cleared* before we made the final arrangements. The Cashier's Check arrived, but there was a catch—it was written

> While the internet has proven to be a convenient way to communicate, it also opens the door to the potential to be defrauded such as phishing.

for quite a bit more then he was paying us. My wife contacted him via email and let him know we had received the check, but it was written for far more than we had agreed upon. He told us he sent extra and asked if we would mind sending the additional funds to the travel agency to pay for his son's trip and some other expenses. He reminded us not to do anything until the money cleared our bank so we would be assured he was on the up and up.

Several things went through our minds, "Why would he take a chance on getting ripped off by sending extra money to people that he doesn't even know? Why would he take a chance on his son's trip getting messed up if we didn't follow through? Why would he make the assumption that we wouldn't mind taking the time to make his son's travel plans--which we thought was pretty bold." Although it was weird, the whole ordeal sounded like it was legit, I mean after all, he did send a Cashier's Check and asked us not to send any money to the travel agency until after it cleared the bank.

I told the story to an acquaintance of mine. He said, "Look out Dave, this sounds like a scam that has been tried on some of my friends that own horses." When I got home, I told my wife Pam," This might be a set up." Pam, who is as smart as she is beautiful, was already on the job. My wife, the detective, got a heavy dose of "women's intuition", and could smell a rat. She decided to get on the internet and get the phone number for the bank whose name was on the Cashier's Check. The person in customer service told Pam he could not find that Cashier's Check number in their data base, but that he would do some investigating and get back to us.

The next morning Pam called again and was told the Cashier's Check was COUNTERFEIT! Wanting to get the details on how something like this would play out, Pam called our local bank. She was shocked to find out this is quite common. The bank representative told her that what happens is someone contacts you regarding something you have for sale, or in this case a service. They proceed to agree with you on a price, usually quite readily, and then they give you a Cashier's Check or Money Order for far more than you agreed. They always ask you to forward the additional funds to someone, usually by Western Union. By sending it Western Union, it can be picked up anywhere in the world, so they can't be tracked.

The bank rep continued to tell Pam that this is when it gets ugly. When a customer whose checking account is in good standing deposits a Cashier's Check, it shows available in their checking account that evening around midnight. It isn't until it comes back to their bank as counterfeit anyone knows there's a problem. This usually takes around 10 DAYS, and by that time it's too late. Of course the victim has already done their part and forwarded the additional funds Western Union! Needless to say, this is when the real heartache begins. Sad but true, cons do not seem to have a conscience when it comes to feathering their nests at the expense of others.

THINGS YOU CAN DO TO HELP PROTECT YOURSELF SAFEGUARDS

- Check your financial accounts for unusual activity
- Keep personal information in a safe place such as your Social Security number, credit card numbers, passwords etc.
- Make sure that you are receiving your bills. If you are not, you may be a victim of the thief changing the address where some of your bills are being sent.
- If you have people coming into your home such as house cleaners, workers, or helpers of any type, keep your personal information secured.
- Complete a background and credit check on any caregivers or assumed professionals who may have access to your personal

information. If you do give access, you will want to read the *How Advisors Can Help* section of this chapter.

- Place passwords on your credit card, bank, and phone accounts. Do not use common information (info that cons look for) such as mother's maiden name, your birth date, the last four digits or your SSN or phone numbers. Also avoid using consecutive numbers. If asked for your mother's maiden name when filling out an application for a new account, try using a password instead.

- If you are going out of town, call the US Postal Service at 1-800-275-8777 and ask for a *vacation hold* on your mail.

- Sending mail that contains sensitive information such as your Social Security number, pin numbers, credit card info etc., should be mailed in post office collection boxes rather than leaving them for pickup in your mailbox at home.

- If you have a computer, put in place safeguards and security features to protect yourself from identity theft.

- If you think that someone may have access to your accounts, contact the following companies for a credit report;
  o Equifax- www.equifax.com or call 1-800-685-1111
  o Experian- www.experian.com or call 1-888-397-3742
  o TransUnion- www.transunion.com or call 1-800-916-8800

- If you believe that fraud has been committed you can place a fraud alert on your credit reports by contacting;
  o Equifax at 1-800-525-6285
  o Experian at 1-888-397-3742
  o TransUnion at 1-800-680-7289

- Close any credit card accounts that the con is using.

- If your bank account has been tampered with, contact your bank, close the account, and tell the bank to notify the appropriate check verification service.

For additional information regarding identity theft you can contact www.consumer.gov/idtheft or call 1-877-438-4338

If you are the victim of fraud you also have this option. In the Bible God warns people about taking advantage of widows and orphans and instructs the victimized widow to cry out to Him. "Do not take advantage of a widow or an orphan. If you do and they cry out to me, I will certainly hear their cry." -Exodus 22:22. Perpetrators may want to read the rest of the verse.

PERSONAL FINANCE HOUSEKEEPING

What are some of the other financial strategies retirees (and all of us for that fact) can use to protect ourselves? Make sure you have the proper *beneficiary designations* on your annuities, life insurance, and IRAs. Don't make the estate the beneficiary unless there are special reasons for doing so. Make sure your assets are *owned correctly* and use tools like living trusts if the estate warrants it…the reason…to help keep your financial information out of probate and therefore out of the public domain. Some state laws require your personal representative to publish a death notice in your local paper. The death notice serves as a public notice of your estate's probate and enables people who think they have an interest (such as creditors) to file a claim against your estate within a specified time period. Scam artists can find your public information and target you for contact.

Employing the right strategies can keep assets out of probate and therefore help curtail phone calls and advances by scam artists who would otherwise not know your financial business. Use *direct deposit* for Social Security and pension checks. Use *automatic bill paying* to keep access away from predators. Or hire a reputable bill paying firm. Besides helping keep your financial information private, a Living Trust can also help protect you if you should become incapacitated.

HOW ADVISORS CAN HELP

What role can an advisor play in helping seniors from becoming victims of a scam? Before employing the following, make sure you have an advisor or advisors with what I call the three "E(s)", *experience, education, and ethics*. Thoroughly check out anyone that you bring into your circle of trust. Once you find people that you are confident you can trust, employing what I call **HELP** can assist you in protecting yourself from potential fraud. I believe it is smart practice to have a team of advisors who you trust such as an attorney (Elder Law and or Estate Planning attorney), CPA (Certified Public Accountant), and a CFP® (Certified Financial Planner). Having more than one advisor, adds another layer of security or you might say, a "check and balance." We have all heard those stories about unethical advisors. If you turn everything over to a sole professional such as a financial advisor, you should thoroughly check them out (see Chapter 6).

H stands for "**hand off to your advisor**". Having a relationship with a qualified advisor is a sound way for seniors to get free from being pressured into having to make financial decisions. If approached to make an investment, loan money, buy insurance or any decision that may affect your finances—even loaning money to a family member—the senior simply says "Here is the number to my financial advisor run it past him and if he thinks it is in my best interest he and I will talk about it."Now what do you think a scam artist will do or a family member up to no good? That's right, they will never call the advisor.

E stands for **evaluation** at least on an annual basis. A trusted advisor can be an excellent resource to provide a check and balance for the senior. What I mean by that is, a family member and/or caregiver can also be perpetrators of a crime against the very family member of the person they are suppose to be helping. If a senior gives someone access to their money or puts them on their bank account as a joint owner (which I usually discourage to protect the parent), the advisor should check all accounts annually to make sure there are no discrepancies. A family member or caregiver resistant to this strategy should alert the senior there may be a problem.

L stands for **liaison**. I recommend that couples find an advisor they are both comfortable working with. One of the main reasons is usually one person in the marriage, be it the husband or the wife, handles the finances in the relationship. What I see happen so often is, when the spouse that controls the finances passes away, the surviving spouse is left in a very vulnerable position. Who does he or she turn to for help? Who can be trusted? Trying to find answers to these questions, while emotions are running high due to a devastating loss, can increase the risk of making bad choices. If the couple had been working with a qualified advisor prior to the loss, a plan could have been put in place to help protect the surviving spouse from possible devastating mistakes.

P stands for **planning.** Without proper planning we can all fall victim to panic. When we are panicked we do not function in a rational way. Therefore, we may put ourselves in a vulnerable position by turning to people who we think have our best interest at heart. We may be afraid of not having enough money to last our lifetime, making us susceptible to those promising *guaranteed high returns on our money with no risk.*

Having a plan in place before a crisis happens puts us in a much better position to ward off those that want to victimize us. A plan can quiet the "what ifs" in our head by answering them before hand so panic doesn't take control when unforeseen events take place. Also, a plan will help guard against solicitations such as charities or investment scams. You can simply say, I have a plan and my money is strategically invested. As it applies to charities, you can tell the caller that you budget annually for charitable

> *Thoroughly check out anyone that you bring into your circle of trust.*

contributions and that the money has already been assigned to causes that are important to you.

SUMMARY

- Be aware of the psychological tools that are sometimes used to take advantage of you. Don't play their game and think that you can win—you are only asking for trouble.

- You have the right to say, "No thank you!" and hang up the phone. Tell the solicitor that you prefer not to be contacted again. If they are reputable they should stop and if not you can go to the internet site www.donotcall.gov requesting that you do not want to be contacted. If they call you back again, you should file a complaint.

- Don't be pressured into acting "now". If you are being pressured, you will be well served to say "no" and politely excuse yourself. As I covered in this chapter the "scarcity" play is to get you to act "now" before the opportunity is gone…don't fall for it.

- Don't click into websites that you do not know for a fact are authentic, and by all means, do not give your password or any financial information.

- Put the *safeguards* in place as discussed in this chapter

- *NEVER* send in money as a prerequisite to pick up your prize. If it's free- it's FREE!

- *NEVER* give your credit card number, social security number or bank account information to an individual that you don't know. Report all suspicious requests to your local law enforcement agency and or any of the contacts that I noted in this chapter.

- Ask for written sales literature or a contract before making decisions. If they tell you that they don't have any or refuse to send it, this should raise a red flag.

- Follow your "gut". If something feels wrong, it probably is.

- Remember that the acronym *HELP* can be just that…help to keep you safe.

- If we bite on any of these scams we are marked as a target. Con criminals step-up the contacts and the pressure knowing that we will most likely take the bait. We would be well served to remember these maxims as it applies to fraud; *if it sounds too good to be true it probably is and an ounce of prevention is worth a pound of cure.*

Chapter 6

What You Need to Know if You Decide Not to Go it Alone

The Sixth Step to a Worry-Free Retirement

If it is serving, let him serve; if it is teaching, let him teach; Romans 12: 6-8

"The beginning of wisdom is silence. The
second step is listening." Unknown

A while back I met with a woman named Ruth. Ruth was self conscious regarding her finances. During our first meeting Ruth was very open about what she owned, but hesitant to talk about where her money was invested. I had a feeling that someone had belittled her regarding past financial decisions. Our conversation went something like this:

David: "Ruth you seem hesitant to share with me where your money is currently invested. In order to determine if I can help you, you need to be comfortable sharing that information with me." **Ruth**: I know that, but I have to admit that I am concerned that you will think that I have made some foolish decisions. I don't want to be embarrassed." **David**: "Why do you think that you will be embarrassed?" **Ruth**: "I met with a financial advisor recently that told me that I have done everything wrong. I felt dumb, and frankly he made me feel stupid. Actually if it wasn't for fear that I have made bad decisions that could affect my future security, I wouldn't be here. I don't want to be humiliated." **David**: "So you called to meet with me because the other advisor made you uncomfortable. Am I correct?" **Ruth**: "Yes, I left his office knowing that I couldn't work with him no matter how smart he was."

Ruth's experience is unfortunately common. I scratch my head in confusion when a new client tells me that their previous financial advisor made them feel foolish for the financial choices that they have made. The fact is, Ruth in her relationships with whomever she chooses as an advisor, is the boss. The advisor works for her….period…end of story. Can you imagine the President or CEO of a company hiring a Chief Financial Officer (CFO) and the CFO saying, "How did you allow such bad business decisions when you had the prior CFO?" The CFO would get his walking papers before he was even introduced to the rest of the company employees.

As the client, if you are to be served as you ought to be, you should be in charge. It is your money. You worked for it, it belongs to you. You call

> *As the client, if you are to be served as you should be, it is important to realize that you are the boss.*

the shots. If the advisor is trying to dominate you, badger you, or control you, he is serving himself or herself and not you. The role of the advisor is to find out what is important to you and how he or she can best help. Ruth felt that she made the best decisions she could at the time with the information she had. She was suspicious that he was trying to make her feel inadequate so she would be dependent on him—which if he succeeded—could make her very vulnerable.

Many of my friends are in the financial planning profession. I am convinced they have their client's best interest at heart. The advisor that made Ruth uncomfortable might have the same heart, but perhaps didn't communicate it like he had hoped to. Occasionally, we as financial advisors do not have the best communication skills. Sometimes we are eager to help, and I for one had to remind myself early on in my career I have two ears and one mouth for a reason. I should be listening more and talking less. Oh…but it was so hard not to anticipate the client's problem and jump in quickly to help save the day! Sadly, it made me feel better to know I wasn't alone and that some of my colleagues had the same challenge. Maybe our desire to become a financial advisor stems from childhood and our need to be needed.

Some years ago a book was popularized that was specifically written to assist financial planners with their communication skills. I read the book and it was very interesting. The authors gave examples of techniques such as pacing and mirroring. Pacing is where one talks at the same rate of speed and tempo with the person that they are communicating with. Mirroring is just what the word implies, which is mirroring the body language of the other person. So for example, if the prospective client leans back in her chair, the advisor does the same and if the prospective client shifts forward so does the advisor. The result of pacing and mirroring is to help the perspective client feel a connection. It is somewhat subliminal. Early on in my career I did use it and it does work. Even though it was effective, I personally felt that I wasn't being myself.

My reason for bringing this up is not to be critical of the technique or the book. I know advisors who use it and are very comfortable with the process. It is not my intention, nor am I qualified to sit in judgment of them. On the contrary, if it helps them communicate better with their client's, then good for them. All I can say is, as for me, it just didn't feel good. Fortunately, my question on how to be a better communicator for my clients was about to be answered.

As an introspective person, I am constantly searching for wisdom. One day when I was reading a chapter in my favorite book, something stopped me in my tracks. What I read changed my life and the relationship with my clients forever. While reading in the Book of Matthew a verse spoken by Jesus jumped off the page; "For out of the overflow of the heart the mouth speaks." (Matthew 12:33-35) The Light came on which helped me realize in the past I had been focusing more on the numbers than the facts. Although I was on target from a technical prospective, something was missing. I discovered that my practice was head focused and not heart focused. Revealed also, was although mirroring and pacing were effective, the process was self-focused not client-focused—at least in my humble opinion. In other words, I was paying more attention on how I should be sitting or talking, rather than listening. This new revelation reenergized me. *I knew that it was my job to listen to my clients and let them speak their hearts.*

What has happened since this clarity is I have been able to help at a level I had never reached before. Sometimes people just want to share their fears, frustrations,

> *I knew that it was my job to listen to my clients and let them speak their hearts.*

doubts, anger and other emotions, not even knowing how they are connected to their money decisions. I didn't need pacing or mirroring anymore. I was reminded of a saying that I read years ago, it went something like this: *the greatest conversations that I have ever had are with people who let me talk about myself.*

You might ask, "All of this might be life changing and interesting for you, but why should I care? Why is this important?" We know the major reason people make poor investment decisions, stems from irrational behavior along with emotions which directly affect behavior. Unless advisors understand the importance of not just gathering facts, but also listening to the emotions of our clients, we may miss getting to core issues. How we feel about money is influenced by our experiences with family, friends, the media, past successes, failures and from other sources that fuel our feelings. Tapping into them helps give us clarity as to why we do what we do financially. I learned that by focusing on my client and not on what I was going to say, helped them open up and discover what was holding them back from making smart money choices. Some clients that I have worked with over the years didn't realize it, but they were actually sabotaging their financial future because of how their emotions toward money were affecting their decisions. Also, by talking about our fears, angers, and other feelings, these negative influences tend to lose their power and control over us resulting in more peace in our lives.

> *What does all of this have to do with choosing an advisor? Plenty…if an advisor is not interested in what we have to say or makes us feel stupid, how can we make rational investment decisions?*

What does all of this have to do with choosing an advisor? Plenty… *if an advisor is not interested in what we have to say or makes us feel stupid, how can we make rational investment decisions?* During her meeting with the prior advisor, Ruth felt belittled and not very important. From their limited discussion, she knew he was self focused and not client focused. Ruth needed to be in an environment where she knew she was the boss and had the right to express herself. Besides being able to express herself, there was also another important reason that she needed to be leery of the advisor that made her uncomfortable: Ruth could have put herself in a vulnerable situation. If Ruth would have been pressured emotionally by the advisor, she may have felt her wishes did not matter or she should not be trusted with her own money. Ruth could have been made to feel she should never question him and that he should be calling the shots…not her. In this situation, Ruth could have been easily taken advantage of.

If you decide that you need an advisor, keep Ruth's story in mind. Look for an advisor that not only has the experience and expertise necessary to help you, but also one with the heart to serve, an environment where you are encouraged to express yourself without judgment, and where you know you are the boss. Feeling safe to talk about your wants, needs, and fears, will help you make smart money choices. Don't choose an advisor lightly. Who you choose may make the difference between financial independence and financial hardship. In addition, consider the following when hiring and working with a financial advisor:

Before you can even begin to seek out a professional, you have to understand what it is you want from a financial planner. Do you need comprehensive planning advice? Do you only need a retirement portfolio review? Are you dealing with business planning issues? Are you concerned about long-term care planning? Different planners have different areas of expertise, so it is very important you find someone who can address your specific situation.

Be wary of someone pushing a product and calling himself a financial advisor or financial planner. "The title of "financial planner" is largely an unregulated term in many countries. Lack of regulation has allowed financial services personnel in these countries to use the title indiscriminately. Often, financial products intermediaries use the title to project a professional image to clients even when they are not trained in the professional aspects of financial planning. This has sometimes led to abuse. Clients may be deceived into choosing financial planning services that are unprofessional, from unethical providers."[2]

Know that some designations can be purchased and don't require additional education or a code of ethics in order to use them. You should know what the various designations mean and what's required of

> *"The title of 'financial planner' is largely an unregulated term in many countries. Lack of regulation has allowed financial services personnel in these countries to use the title indiscriminately.*

a person using them. Contact the issuing organizations directly to obtain what education and experience is required to obtain the designation as well as the code of ethics and continuing education required for the practitioner to be able to use the designation. (Contact information for the various issuing organizations follows.)

Find out if the advisor has had any ethics violations or license revocations or suspensions. If the advisor is securities licensed, you can check his/her status by contacting the National Association of Securities Dealers (NASD) at 301-590-6500 or on their Web site www.nasd.com. If an advisor is insurance licensed, check with the Department of Insurance in your state. If he/she has professional designations, you can check with the issuing organization. The more common designations have codes of ethics and require various levels of education. To check about a Certified Financial Planner (CFP®), contact the Certified Financial Planner Board of Standards at 303-830-7543. For a Certified Senior Advisor (CSA), contact the Society of Certified Senior Advisors at 800-653-1785. To check on a Chartered Life Underwriter (CLU) or Chartered Financial Consultant (ChFC), call the American College at 888-AMERCOL (888-263-7265).

If creating a financial plan is free of charge, keep in mind the old saying that there is no free lunch; in order for the advisor to make a living, you will have to buy something. A financial plan should stand on its own without representing any financial products. I believe you *can* get objective advice from someone who receives income only from commissions, but you must understand that's how the advisor's compensation is determined before your plan is created. Take to heart this wise saying, *free advice may be the most expensive advice that you ever receive.*

Choose an advisor with the right focus for you. When clients come to me, I tell them my area of expertise and how I work with clients. If they are looking for someone with a different focus or expertise, I'll guide them to an advisor more suited to their needs. Finding an advisor who is right for you might take some research and a few interviews.

Realize that any savings or investment plans you get involved in will always have an upside and downside. No investment or savings plan is perfect. Your advisor should make sure you know the positives and negatives of any financial decisions you make. For example, when you put your money in a certificate of deposit, you're giving up interest on your money for security. If you invest in stocks, you're giving up safety for the potential of a better return. Understand what you are investing in. You should be solving a problem not creating one.

Never loan money to a financial advisor or invest in a firm that's owned or controlled by the advisor. These are ethics violations. If you are ever asked to do either,

> *Realize that any savings or investment plans you get involved in will always have an upside and downside. No investment or savings plan is perfect.*

you should report the advisor—if the advisor is an insurance agent, call the Department of Insurance in your state, or contact NASD if he or she is a registered representative. Then find another advisor.

Your advisor should focus on you. Your advisor should provide you with all the information necessary to make an informed decision, and you should never feel rushed. If your advisor is trying to rush you, he's probably working in his own best interest, not yours. It may be necessary to meet you're your advisor several times where you ask questions and your advisor guides and educates you before you feel comfortable making a decision. Your advisor should be willing to spend the time to accomplish that objective.

Work with an advisor who has many arrows in his/her quiver. Funny isn't it, how an advisor who sells only whole life insurance, for instance, will discover that someone who needs a financial product needs whole life insurance? Whole life might be right for you or it might be wrong. The point is that your advisor should be working on your behalf to find the right product and right product manufacturer to meet your needs. If your advisor has only a hammer, then everything looks like a nail. Don't get nailed with bad advice. Make sure that the person whom you entrust with your money is looking out for your needs.

You must be willing to share your personal financial information with your advisor if you expect him or her to do a quality job for you. Your advisor must be privy to your tax status, investment objectives, risk tolerance, time horizon, and other information specific to your situation. Otherwise, his recommendations may not be suitable for your needs.

Make sure your advisor is qualified to help you. The new retirement culture calls for specialized experience and education. He or she should have experience and expertise in the following areas:

➤ long-term care

➤ asset allocation

➤ how to help insure income for life

➤ tax saving efficiencies

➤ legal tools

➤ ownership and beneficiary designations to protect assets and survivor income

Interview the prospective advisor before you decide on hiring that person. You will be working closely together and sharing your personal information. So unless you are confident that the advisor is right for

> *Make sure your advisor is qualified to help you. The new retirement culture calls for specialized experience and education.*

you, do not hesitate to keep looking. Your financial well being may depend upon it.

How about doing your own financial planning? Some personal finance software packages, magazines or self-help books can help you do your own financial planning. However, you may decide to seek help from a professional financial planner if:

• You need expertise you don't possess in certain areas of your finances. For example, a planner can help you evaluate the level of risk in your investment portfolio or help you determine the rate of return you need to stay financially independent.

• You or your spouse is in need of long-term care and you want to know the smartest way to pay for it.

• You want to get a professional opinion about the financial plan you developed for yourself.

- You don't feel you have the time to spare to do your own financial planning, or you need a second opinion.

- You have an immediate need or unexpected life event such as a death, inheritance or major illness.

- You are not sure you are doing things right and you need guidance.

- You know that you need to make financial changes but don't know where to start.

- You are not sure that you own your assets correctly to protect yourself from disinheritance, major illness, or transferring your money to your loved ones without unnecessary cost, delay, and taxes.

My intention in writing this chapter is not to disparage my colleagues or to make you fearful of financial planners. From my experience, there are far more ethical and caring advisors out there than ones that are only out for themselves. It is my hope this chapter will help guard you from making possible mistakes that can detrimentally affect your financial future; using the information to guide you to the right planner. I conclude this chapter with some information from the Certified Financial Planner Board of Standards that I think may be very helpful for you.

THE FOLLOWING IS FROM THE CERTIFIED FINANCIAL PLANNER BOARD OF STANDARDS

"In addition to providing you with general financial planning services, many financial planners are also registered as investment advisers or hold insurance or securities licenses that allow them to buy or sell products. Other planners may have you use more specialized financial advisers to help you implement their recommendations. With the right education and experience, each of the following advisers could take you through the financial planning process. Ethical financial planners will refer you to one of these professionals for services that they cannot provide and disclose any referral fees they may receive in the process. Similarly, these advisers should refer you to a planner if they cannot meet your financial planning needs."

The following is a list of advisers that you may need, and the roles that they play.

Accountant

Accountants provide you with advice on tax matters and help you prepare and submit your tax returns to the Internal Revenue Service. All accountants who practice as Certified Public Accountants (CPAs) must be licensed by the state(s) in which they practice.

Estate Planner

Estate planners provide you with advice on estate taxes or other estate planning issues and put together a strategy to manage your assets at the time of your death. While attorneys, accountants, financial planners, insurance agents or trust bankers may all provide estate planning services, you should seek an attorney to prepare legal documents such as wills, trusts and powers of attorney. Many estate planners hold the Accredited Estate Planner (AEP) designation.

Financial Planner

Many financial planners have earned the CERTIFIED FINANCIAL PLANNER™ certification, or the Chartered Financial Consultant (ChFC) or Personal Financial Specialist (CPA/PFS) designations. Financial planners can take you through the financial planning process.

Insurance Agent

Insurance agents are licensed by the state(s) in which they practice to sell life, health, property and casualty or other insurance products. Many insurance agents hold the Chartered Life Underwriter (CLU) designation. Financial planners may identify and advise you on your insurance needs, but can only sell you insurance products if they are also licensed as insurance agents.

Investment Adviser

Anybody who is paid to provide securities advice must register as an investment adviser with the Securities and Exchange Commission or relevant state securities agencies, depending on the amount of money he or she manages. Because financial planners often advise people on securities-based investments, many are registered as investment advisers. Investment advisers cannot sell securities products without a securities license. For that, you must use a licensed securities representative such as a stockbroker.

Stockbroker

Also called registered representatives, stockbrokers are licensed by the state(s) in which they practice to buy and sell securities products such as stocks, bonds and mutual funds. They generally earn commissions on all of their transactions. Stockbrokers must be registered with a company that is a member of the National Association of Securities Dealers (NASD) and pass NASD-administered securities exams.

CFP Board's free brochure, *10 Questions to Ask When Choosing a Financial Planner*, can help you look for someone who is qualified to offer financial planning advice. CFP Board's Web site, www.CFP.net/learn, is a comprehensive resource that can help you find a financial advisor.

BEST PRACTICES WHEN APPROACHING FINANCIAL PLANNING

- Set measurable goals.
- Understand the effect your financial decisions have on other financial issues.
- Re-evaluate your financial plan periodically.
- Start now - don't assume financial planning is for when you get older.
- Start with what you've got - don't assume financial planning is only for the wealthy.
- Take charge - you are in control of the financial planning engagement.
- Look at the big picture - financial planning is more than just retirement planning or tax planning.
- Don't confuse financial planning with investing.
- Don't expect unrealistic returns on investments.
- Don't wait until a money crisis to begin financial planning.

SUMMARY

- Remember, you are the boss. *The advisor works for you.*
- Choosing an environment where you are free to express your fears, desires and anger, along with any other emotions without judgment, will give you greater opportunity to succeed.
- Look for someone with the expertise and experience that you need.
- Interview a variety of advisors until you know one is right for you

Chapter 7

Where Do You Go From Here

The Seventh Step to a Worry-Free Retirement

"Always plan ahead. It wasn't raining when Noah
built the ark." Richard C. Cushing

"For the great gain of education is not knowledge
but action." Herbert Spencer

A couple that I will call Phil and Lois came to see me. Having never met them before, as with all of my introductory meetings, I was there to listen and find out how they were hoping I could help them. Phil had a look of worry on his face. He looked like a man under stress. As he and Lois spoke with me, I was starting to understand why. Phil was raised in a culture that strongly believed the man should be responsible for the family's finances. He worked hard at his profession as a plant manager and had been a good provider. Phil's expression showed the strain of entering a new phase in his life: transitioning from working to pay the bills to now investing to provide a comfortable lifestyle for him and Lois. Phil worried if he made a mistake at this time in their lives, they could not earn back their savings they worked so hard to accumulate and therefore a misstep would be catastrophic.

This new hat was obviously uncomfortable for Phil. Adding to his stress; they had recently attended an investment seminar that raised more questions than answers. Unfortunately, both Phil and Lois left the seminar confused about how to navigate the future. The problem was the seminar speakers talked about an array of investment options which made their heads spin. In addition, they told me they didn't understand some of the investment terms that were used. They attended the seminar because they simply wanted to invest their money for retirement not to take a class on a multitude of investment terms.

What Phil and Lois were hoping I could do for them was to provide clarity and reassurance. They wanted a simple solution to a complex process. I told them the same thing that I have shared with you in this book, and that is, without a plan not only would they be shooting in the dark but so would their advisor. Without a plan to direct them along with the person or team assisting, they might as well flip a coin and hope for the best. The point that I am trying to make is this, they were about to go down an investment trail making the mistake that so many investors make: *they were falling in the trap of investing their money before investing their time in mapping out their future.* Once they map out where they are and where they want to go, they can take action to get there with confidence. In other words, they must first determine their need and then choose the right investment to meet it…not the other way around.

In his book *Age Power*, Dr. Ken Dychtwald puts it like this, "Lacking proactive planning, many elders wind up depleting their life savings—and their children's inheritance—as they tumble into poverty."[4] Who wants that? So, then why don't more people plan? Don't get mad at me gentlemen but I do have to put much of the blame on us guys for not planning our financial futures. Either we don't want a financial advisor nosing in our business, or we believe we can do it ourselves, (even though 78% of us don't do it). Then again, we are the ones that think we can drive our car to any destination and we don't even need a map…right? I haven't done the research but I don't think it is a stretch to believe that if it weren't for women, there would not be a market for cars with navigation devices. My view is supported by the comedian, Jeff Foxworthy. On the show "Are You Smarter Then a 5th Grader", Mr. Foxworthy asked the contestant, "Who was the first American astronaut to orbit the earth?" The contestant answered correctly, "John Glenn". Mr. Foxworthy quipped, "Did you know that he orbited three times and the

> *"Lacking proactive planning, many elders wind up depleting their life savings— and their children's inheritance—as they tumble into poverty"*

reason he did …because like most men he didn't check his map?"

As I wrote about in the investment chapter, no wonder we lose courage and change course…we don't know where we are headed. A financial plan is a must in order to help us map a destination, navigate the rough waters *that will happen* and stay the course. You may be saying, "Okay David you made your point, we know that we need to plan; so then where do we go from here?" Here are the steps:

1. Set your goals. Ask yourself: what type of lifestyle you want to maintain and how much income do you need to maintain it? What are your irregular expenses such as: buying a new car every x number of years; grandchildren's cost of education; household goods; vacations etc. List any other financial goals.

2. Decide if you want to hire an advisor(s) or try to go it alone. If you decide to go with an advisor(s) please refer to Chapter 6.

3. Once you have chosen an advisor(s) you will need to invest some time to build a plan. You may need to meet with your advisor(s) several times. This is not a process of mechanically imputing data in a spreadsheet and out pops a plan. Many times the plan needs to be modified until it is the right fit. You will know when the plan is correct for you. Everyone's situation is different and this is a very personal process.

   I thoroughly enjoy this part of working with clients; it gives them time to focus on themselves and their needs. I don't know about you, but I enjoy talking about myself on occasion (my family is probably saying, "What do you mean on occasion, how about all of the time?"), but this time is for my clients to talk about what is important to them. I need to point out here if your objective is for you and your spouse to navigate the retirement waters together; you will both need to attend the meetings. Done individually, the result can create discord. I have found even if either the husband or wife makes the decisions, they both need to be involved. (An exception is when one spouse suffers from dementia or a form of dementia called Alzheimer's). I believe that each person's concerns, needs, and desires should be equally respected.

   Many times people do not think about the vulnerability of a surviving spouse when one of them passes away. The fact is a grieving person can be targeted by predators. Also, they are susceptible to making bad decisions. When people plan together, they have peace of mind knowing when one of them passes away the surviving spouse has the security of a trusting and respectful relationship, assuming you are working with the right advisor(s). In other words you know your spouse will be cared for by someone that cares for him or her. In addition, the surviving spouse will have a road map that both helped put together.

Make sure that your plan addresses all the risks associated with living longer, which are:

o   If either or both of you should need long-term care, what is your financial risk exposure? If you do have financial risk, what is the most efficient and cost effective way to reduce or eliminate the risk?

o   Do you and your spouse have enough money to maintain purchasing power throughout your life expectancy?

o   What are the smart investment choices you need to make?

o   What is the right asset allocation model for you?

o   Is your money positioned correctly?

o   Are you paying more in taxes than the government requires? Which assets should you use first to create income?

4.   Have your plan reviewed annually to keep things up to date and to modify where necessary.

For those of you saying to yourself, "I know this is important if I am to achieve my goal to live with independence and dignity in my remaining years, but I can't find time to plan right now." If that is you, I will leave you with this: most of us have probably heard the story about a man that wanted to quit procrastinating. Motivated, he signed up to take a class called procrastinator's anonymous. He was never able to attend because every time the man showed up for the meeting the sign on the door read, "Meeting moved to next week at the same time."

Opting to put off today for what we can do tomorrow is easy for all of us. Dave Ramsey, in his book titled *The Total Money Makeover*, says it like it is; it is a myth to believe, "I don't have time to work on a budget, retirement plan, or estate plan. The truth is you don't have time not to." Knowing what you now know to protect yourself from the threat of longevity risk will not do you one ounce of good if you don't take action.

Not very long ago a client who had put off planning told me, now because of planning, she can sleep better and her life is more enjoyable. Another client

> *"Inaction breeds doubt and fear. Action breeds confidence and courage. If you want to conquer fear, do not sit home and think about it. Go out and get busy." Dale Carnegie*

shared with me, prior to planning, she was walking blindly into the future not knowing what may lie ahead that could rob her of her independence. People are frequently astonished at the peace of mind that planning has given them. Many have shared they didn't plan because they were afraid of what they might find out. Like most anything in life, fear can hold us back and cripple us from doing what we know we should. Dale Carnegie put it like this, "Inaction breeds doubt and fear. Action breeds confidence and courage. If you want to conquer fear, do not sit home and think about it. Go out and get busy."

We can certainly apply Mr. Carnegie's wisdom to financial planning…*we need to get busy*. Who doesn't want to control fear instead of fear controlling us and who doesn't want to have more confidence? So as the famous Nike slogan says—"*just do it*." If you don't do it for you, do it for those that you love. May God bless your efforts.

Notes

1   The Kaiser Commission on Long-term care
2   Wikipedia August 2007
3   Williams, C. "Profiles of Nursing Home Residents on Medicaid," conducted by AZA Consulting for the KCMU
4   Ken Dychtwald, Ph.D. "*Age Power*"
5   Scott L. Lummer, Ph.D., CFA and Mark W. Riepe, CFA, "*The Role of Asset Allocation in Portfolio Management*." John Wiley & Sons, 1994
6   Ibbotson Associates. (Ibbotson SBBI classic yearbook) "*Stocks, Bonds, Bills and Inflation*" 2007 edition.
7   David R. Babbel, Craig B. Merrill, "*Investing your Lump Sum at Retirement*". Wharton Financial Institutions Center Policy Brief: Personal Finance, August 14, 2007
8   Paul D. Kaplan, "*Asset Allocation With Annuities For Retirement Income Management*". Insurance Newsnet, 2006.
9   Jeffrey R. Brown, "The New Retirement Challenge". *Tax Analysts*, 2004
10   Brinson, Gary P., L. Randolph Hood, and Gilbert L. Beebower. 1986. "Determinants of Portfolio Performance." *Financial Analysts Journal*, vol. 42, no 4 (July/August):39-48.
11   AARP Off the Hook: "*Reducing Participation in Telemarketing Fraud*"
12   Trudy Lieberman, *Consumer Reports Complete Guide to Health Services for Seniors*, page 237.)
13   Marilee Driscoll, "*The Complete IDIOT'S Guide to Long-Term Care Planning*": *Consumer Reports Complete Guide to Health Services* for

Seniors by Trudy Lieberman and Editors of Consumer Reports; J.K Lasser's *Choosing the Right Long-Term Care Insurance, Difficult Decisions Made Easy by* Benjamin Lipson*; Long-Term Care Insurance Made Simple* by Les Abromovitz

14 John Ameriks, Ph.D., Robert Veres, Mark Warshawsky, Ph.D, "Making Retirement Income Last a Lifetime." *Journal of Financial Planning*, December 2001, Article 6

15 Fidelity Investments

Index

W